How to Romance
the Man You Love—The Way
He Wants You To!

How to Romance the Man You Love—The Way He Wants You To!

Lucy Sanna

THREE RIVERS PRESS • NEW YORK

Published by Three Rivers Press, New York, New York.
Member of the Crown Publishing Group, a division of Random House, Inc.
www.crownpublishing.com

THREE RIVERS PRESS and the Tugboat design are registered trademarks of Random House, Inc.

Originally published by Prima Publishing, Roseville, California, in 2001.
Previously published in hardcover by Prima Publishing, Roseville, California, in 1996.

Grateful acknowledgment is made to the following for permission to excerpt material:
New Male Sexuality, by Bernie Zilbergeld, Ph.D. Copyright © 1992 by Bernie Zilbergeld. Used by permission of Bantam Books, a division of Bantam Doubleday Dell Publishing Group, Inc.

The Men We Never Knew, by Daphne Rose Kingma. Copyright © 1994 by Daphne Rose Kingma. Reprinted by permission of Conari Press.

You Just Don't Understand, by Deborah Tannen, Ph.D. Copyright © 1990 by Deborah Tannen, Ph.D. By permission of William Morrow and Company, Inc.

Men Are from Mars, Women Are from Venus, by John Gray. Copyright © 1992 by John Gray. Reprinted by permission of HarperCollins Publishers, Inc.

Mars and Venus in the Bedroom, by John Gray. Copyright © 1995 by JG Productions, Inc. Reprinted by permission of HarperCollins Publishers, Inc. For additional rights/territory, contact Patti Breitman, 12 Rally Court, Fairfax, CA 94930.

Mr. Bridge, by Evan S. Connell. Copyright © 1969 by Evan S. Connell. Reprinted by permission of Alfred A. Knopf/Random House, Inc.

Printed in the United States of America

Library of Congress Cataloging-in-Publication Data
Sanna, Lucy.
How to romance the man you love—the way he wants you to / Lucy Sanna.
p. cm.
Includes bibliographical references and index.
1. Man-woman relationships. 2. Intimacy (Psychology). 3. Love.
4. Men—Psychology. I. Title.
HQ801.S4337 1995
306.7—dc20   94-23778

ISBN 0-7615-0869-4

10 9 8 7

First Edition

To my parents,
Charles Albert and Margaret McGee Sanna,
on their fiftieth wedding anniversary

Contents

Acknowledgments

To the many men who opened up their lives to me, giving me permission to share their feelings and ideas, I am truly grateful. Besides those I personally interviewed, I thank the hundreds of men who responded to an anonymous survey—either by surface mail or by electronic mail through the World Wide Web—for they provided the critical data that give the book honesty and substance

I am particularly grateful to those individuals who took special time and care to personally assist and advise me through project development:

Dr. Gerald Smith, who brought his many years of professional experience as a couples therapist to bear upon the survey as well as upon the content of the book.

Bob Kubik, who provided guidance on the content of the final draft and also introduced me to a very special men's group—Hobie Wright, Dennis Luftig, Steve Marshall, David Bunnett, David Lubin—who together offered valuable insight.

David Dietrich, who provided ideas throughout the development process as well as editorial expertise on the final draft.

Tony Berumen, who developed the software program for capturing data from the extensive ninety-four-question survey.

Members of my family who supported me in various ways throughout the project, including my sisters and brothers—Mary Sanna and Eric James, John and Pat Sanna, Mike and Pam Sanna—as well as my daughter, Katherine Frisch, who on her summer vacation painstakingly input hundreds of survey responses.

Individuals at Prima Publishing who took special interest in this project, most importantly Alice Anderson, Steven Martin, and Frank Ruiz.

Many friends, associates, and cheerleaders who provided support throughout the process, including Stephanie Cincotta, Cherie Minor, Agueda Alverez, Leslie Lamarre, Kathy Miller, Peter Jaret, Stephen Peterson, and especially Heinz Oetiker, who on that winding road through the Swiss Alps got me started.

Introduction

On the face of it, romance seems pretty simple: You and your partner strive to please each other in every way you know how.

All too often, however, a woman bases her actions upon what she herself would like. But is that what *he* wants?

Ask a woman to define romance, and she may describe an atmosphere of passion that would take your breath away. Or she may get misty-eyed as she recounts a tragic drama, where two lovers are separated by circumstances but remain true, willing to die for their love.

Ask a man what romance means, and he'll say, "Work!" That's because it has traditionally been the man's "job" to romance the woman. But change the question to, How would you want a woman to romance you? and the man will give you a raised eyebrow, a sly smile, and a very different response.

Do Men Want Romance?

While developing the survey for this book, I conducted extensive interviews with men, and in the process I found that men are truly confused about romance. One man went so far as to seek out a dictionary definition of the word before he would even discuss the subject. And another man joked, "Just give us good food and good sex, and we're happy"—the expected macho response—until he realized that I was serious.

Whether or not they understand the meaning of *romance*, hundreds of men demonstrated, in an extensive, nationwide survey, that they do want those aspects of a love relationship that may be defined as romantic. And the responses were very consistent.

The ninety-four-question survey was distributed to men through the mail, as well as offered electronically on the Internet, and because the survey was anonymous, respondents were surprisingly candid and comprehensive in answering open-ended questions. It was from such answers that I garnered most of the quotes used throughout this book. Other quotes came from interviews. While the appendix at the back of the book provides an overview of the survey results, the chapters themselves both analyze and provide options for responding to the needs men expressed.

The Romantic Response

Of course you want to please the man you love, because, well, you love him. But you'll be glad to know that there is a lot in it for you as well. Like the women who answered the survey for my earlier book *How to Romance the Woman You Love—The Way She Wants You To!,* men who responded to this survey said they are more inclined to please their partners when they themselves receive the romantic attention that they want. In other words, if you romance your partner his way, he will be more receptive to fulfilling *your* desires.

Through my research, not only did I learn what men want in romance, I also learned how well women are satisfying men's romantic needs. And I found that many well-meaning women do not know how to please their own sweetheart.

Unfortunately, women make a lot of assumptions about what their partner does and does not want. According to hundreds of men across the United States, we women are trying to romance men on our terms. We want lots of attention, so he must want lots of attention. We want to talk about our day, so let's get him to talk about his day. We can take a hint about what he wants, so he should be able to figure out what we want.

True?

To interpret survey responses, I sought the counsel of Dr. Gerald Smith, a psychologist practicing in San Mateo, California. Since 1966, Smith has held workshops at Esalen Institute in Big Sur, California, for couples who already have a good relationship but want to have an even better one. He calls these workshops "Keeping a Good Relationship Alive." Hence he's had the opportunity to work with hundreds of couples who in various ways have become quite skilled at romancing one another.

According to Smith, many men have a hard time expressing what they want because they don't actually know what they feel. This may come as a surprise to women, who are generally so close to their own feelings and rarely have trouble expressing them. Unlike women, men have been taught to suppress their feelings, deny their hurt, and forgo needs. Smith claims that most men have a "delay system in our electrical wiring in what we feel." Feelings may come out an hour or a day later. In contrast, what women feel on the inside tends to correspond with what they express on the outside.

"Men know what they want in terms of outcomes," says Smith. "They want to feel good. They want to feel wanted. But they don't think much in terms of process, how to get it to happen. And when you're making an inquiry about romance, you're asking men to take a look at how they feel and how they want to feel. And so it really requires skillful interviewing to find that out because you're into a mystery land."

So how can a woman discover her partner's romantic needs?

According to Smith, one of the best ways to learn what your partner wants is through play. Playing games allows both partners to let down their defenses and become more vulnerable to each other, which is key to an open relationship. Once a woman begins to discover her partner's needs and desires through play, she can try different methods for satisfying them. Following Smith's suggestions, I've incorporated play throughout this book, mainly in the numerous ideas, activities, and exercises that will help you decipher how to please your own partner. If you begin with the exercises that you find most comfortable, you may gradually gain the confidence to take greater risks.

One reason play is so useful is that it's based on the premise that the two players are functioning as equals. The model of equality as "separate and different but equal" is a good model for a love relationship. A relationship of equality offers the best possibility for individual growth as well as for intimacy.

Because the survey was anonymous, the results are quite revealing. Just knowing what men in general desire from a romantic relationship will help to raise your awareness of your own partner's desires. But it is important to note that the ways to fulfill male desires differ widely. For that reason, you must know specifically what your own partner wants and how best to please him.

To help you tailor your approach, chapter 9, "Deciphering His Desires," includes a detailed checklist for you to use as a guide in learning your own partner's preferences. If you follow through on information gathered, you will not only learn how to please your partner in more personal and intimate ways, but you will also bring a new romantic warmth to your relationship as a whole.

Men are not accustomed to being romanced, so even if you attempt just a few of the exercises in each chapter, you will not only raise your partner's romance awareness, but you will probably knock his socks off!

Now is the time to start—whether you've just met that terrific guy or whether you've been married for years and years. Get to know your partner better. Let him see a more romantic you. After all, you want this romance to remain vital far into the future. The fact that you picked up this book indicates your interest in pleasing your partner and enhancing the quality of your relationship, so you're already on your way.

Expectation, Resentment, and Guilt

Romancing your partner requires an open mind as well as an open heart.

Think back to that wonderfully romantic courting period, when you and your partner were just getting to know each other. You ran to your love with open arms and expected so much in return. You brushed aside his shortcomings, and you found his odd mannerisms endearing. You weren't aware of his personal problems, his bad habits, or even his wonderful capacity to please. In other words, you probably didn't know him as well as you do now. You hoped for the best—but you expected even more. And guess what? He may have expected things from you that would have caused you embarrassment and doubt had you only known.

Expectations are not agreements. On the contrary. In the words of one man I interviewed, "Expectations are premeditated resentments." We come to resent not receiving what we expected to be ours.

Such resentments may not only grow into a wedge between two otherwise loving partners, they may also cause feelings of guilt. If you harbor resentments, your partner may feel like the defendant in Kafka's *The Trial:* He is vaguely charged with an unnamed crime. He knows he is probably guilty. But he is not sure what he has done wrong. This is not romantic.

Your first step in romance is to forgive your partner for not meeting all of your expectations. This isn't something you need to express to him verbally, for that may serve only to heighten his feelings of guilt and inadequacy. This is something you must confess to yourself. And what you will receive in return is joy—the joy that comes with an open heart.

Take a few minutes now to think through some of your unmet expectations. Once you're aware of having them, you will be more likely to recognize them as they occur over the coming days and weeks. When you do, smile to yourself and practice forgiveness. Let them go, take a deep breath, and begin again.

Know Yourself

This book focuses on pleasing the man you love, and it provides lots of ideas and tools to help you do that. But while attempting to satisfy your partner's desires, it is imperative that you do not lose sight of your own integrity, identity, and self-respect. You do not want to later resent something you did or allowed to happen only for the sake of pleasing your partner. That certainly would not make for a romantic relationship.

Every woman is unique. What you want is not exactly what your best friend wants. You are pleased in ways that may differ from those that please your sister. You are not willing to do some of the things that the woman down the street may be willing to do. You are your own person.

If you feel embarrassed, offended, or otherwise compromised by something that your partner wants you to do, don't do it. If you don't feel comfortable wearing revealing lingerie, giving your partner a massage, or even polishing his shoes, don't. As you will see from the numerous exercises suggested throughout this book, there are so many ways you can both stimulate and satisfy your partner's romantic desires. It's up to you to choose those that best fit your own romantic philosophy.

"But I thought this book was about romance," you say. "How can saying *no* be romantic?"

If you say yes to something you don't want to do, you will build up resentment that will eventually come between you and your partner. Moreover, you won't fool him; he'll know right away that you're not having fun. Keep in mind that your partner wants you to be happy. And if you're not happy, he feels that it's his fault. So make sure that what you do for him also makes you happy, and let him take some of the credit for your happiness. If you can please your partner in ways that also please you, you've got a lot of romance coming.

The chapters that follow are filled with ideas that men across the country thought would increase the romance in their own love relationships. Some of these ideas will not be for you. Others may be possibilities to put on the back burner for a while, to simmer a bit.

That's not to say that you shouldn't experiment a little. In the survey, men said they would love to see their partner take a few more risks, try a few new things, be a little more creative in the romance department. Trying something new may be uncomfortable at first, but with small successes, you may start to enjoy initiating romance. Life's too short to stay in that little box. Break out, and increase the romance for both of you.

The key is to start by trying the exercises that fit you most comfortably, and then gradually build on what you learn— what you learn about what pleases you as well as what pleases your partner. This is how to expand your romantic spirit.

And as your relationship becomes more and more romantic, you'll find your comfort level rising, and you just may become more willing to experiment with new activities and techniques. From a man's point of view, *that* is romantic.

Getting Your Partner Involved

If you believe that your relationship would benefit from you and your partner sharing this book or its companion volume (on romancing the woman he loves), try getting him involved by letting him know your wishes for a more romantic relationship. Instead of telling him what he should do, however, express your ideas in terms of what you would like. For example, instead of saying, "I think this book would be good for you," a more romantic suggestion would be, "These books have some fun things for us to try together. How about doing some of them with me?"

If he appears uninterested at first, don't let that stop you from initiating the fun. He'll catch on quickly. And then he'll want to know where to go to enhance his own repertoire of romantic ideas.

Maintain the Momentum

It's easy to let the trivialities of daily life get in the way of romance, but if you can do at least one little romantic thing for your partner each day, you will foster increasing intimacy in your relationship.

Be persistent. If your partner doesn't notice the "new romantic you" right away, don't despair. Eventually, he *will* notice. And when he does, you can be sure that he'll come right back at you with some pretty terrific romantic moves of his own. So be prepared. Whenever he makes the smallest attempt to romance you, respond positively. Every time he does something that puts the two of you on the road to a happier relationship, notice it; tell him you appreciate it. That way he'll learn what pleases *you*.

Be sure to give yourself (and your partner) credit for progress, no matter how small. Congratulate yourself. Celebrate!

Keep it up, expand it, delight in it.

1

Meet the Warrior in Transition

There once was a woman who fell in love. She ran to her new love with open arms and open heart, and she gave him her best time, her best thoughts, and lots and lots of energy. The joy in her love was so profound that she was willing to sacrifice everything for him. And so she sacrificed her individuality for the relationship, her personal friends for mutual friends, and her personal time doing what she wanted to do for time doing what they as a couple wanted to do.

After a few years, she felt that she was doing all the work to keep the relationship going. She was still giving her best time, her best thoughts, and lots and lots of energy. And her partner was merely going to work every day and coming home, expecting her to be happy.

"I don't feel loved," she said to the man.

"But I'm doing all these things for you," he said. "I go to work every morning. I play with the children when I come home. I fix things around the house on the weekends."

"You're not doing these things for me," she answered. "You're doing them because they need to be done. You would do them whether or not I was in your life. This does not help me feel loved."

So much of what we see depends on where we are standing when we look. Although we know what we're giving, we don't know what is received.

1

Valuing His Manhood

Partly in response to the feminist movement that began sweeping the country in the 1970s, a flurry of male-authored books were published to variously question, defend, explain, celebrate, and/or raise the consciousness of Western man.

Robert Bly's *Iron John,* however, was quickly followed by a very silly *Dating Iron John,* while Sam Keen's *Fire in the Belly* was mocked with *Fire in the John.* Doesn't anyone take men seriously?

More recently, in the introduction to his book *The New Male Sexuality,* Dr. Bernie Zilbergeld, a practicing psychologist specializing in men's issues, tries to put into perspective the male dilemma that has arisen from the social change of the last few decades:

> Yes, a man should still be strong, but this should be balanced by sensitivity and restraint. Too much strength is now paradoxically seen as a defect, a sign of neurosis. The term *macho* is used today as often in a derogatory sense as in an admiring one. And a man has to be careful about the sensitivity, as well. Too much of it, however much that may be, can get him called wimp and weakling. Yes, a man should still be successful at work, but somehow he should also find time to relate to his partner and participate equally in child-rearing and household chores. Exactly where the time and energy will come from to carry out all these tasks is never explained. Yes, a man should still be a forceful lover. After all, women don't want wimps in bed. But in addition he should be tender and considerate, understanding his partner's desires and rhythms even though she may not speak them, and be willing to do whatever is necessary for her satisfaction. Yes, a man should still take the sexual initiative, and he should persevere even when he encounters slight or possibly feigned resistance. But now he needs to differentiate possibly feigned resistance from a genuine rebuff, and he needs to be careful lest a sexual invitation he makes is construed as sexual harassment.

Of course, we might be able to poke a few holes in this. As the famous ballroom dancer Ginger Rogers once said, "Women do it in high heels and backwards." Yet if we want to romance that guy we love, we better know where he's coming from. And it's not a pretty place.

According to Dr. Gerald Smith, a practicing psychologist who has been conducting couples workshops for thirty years, "We all came from the cave. Men and women both had ways of operating to survive. The essentially male fight-or-flight response is directly related to the cave. And those ways are imprinted at a very primitive level. The men who made themselves vulnerable back in the cave got killed. Those who wanted to sit around and talk about things got eaten. And, of course, those who survived passed on their survival response genes to their sons."

Men have traditionally been raised to be warriors, protecting women and children. How can we ask them to go to war for us, to protect us in the night, to shield us from the danger that may lurk in an alley, and still to show us their vulnerabilities? If a man shakes in his boots, he is a sissy. If he shrinks from a fight, he's a coward. If he tells secrets, he's a traitor. By emoting, a man can quickly lose friends, career, and self-esteem.

Over the past two decades, the women's movement has changed some of this. As women assumed roles that were once exclusively male, men began to let go of that all-consuming requirement to show only hardened strength. More and more men today are serving the family dinner, comforting the sick child, and doing the household laundry.

But we still see the warrior image all around us. For many young men, the motto splashed across T-shirts and pickup truck windows is "No fear." Toy guns and soldiers (in such forms as Power Rangers) are still popular with boys. Teenage boys flock to theaters that show films filled with violence and destruction, where the "hero" succeeds in overcoming all odds without so much as a wince. And even the little boy whose parents refuse to let him watch violence on TV or play with war toys may one day be called upon to defend home and country, wives and children, or maybe just his little sister from the school bully. In Western society, the fact is that boys and men continue to hold the front, protecting us all.

So it's hardly surprising that men are reticent when it comes to opening up. Hardened by popular images and expectations, many men have lost track of their feelings. Unfortunately, as a result, women feel left out, estranged, and emotionally abandoned when their partners won't express their fears and desires. To this, Zilbergeld writes:

> Males are the ones who are forced to suppress huge parts of themselves, the softer and vulnerable aspects. While this is usually heard as a complaint from women, there is little recognition of how men suffer because of it. They are the ones who aren't able to get hugged or comforted, who can't physically or verbally express the love they feel for male friends they may have known for half a lifetime, who can't find release and relief through tears, who can't openly admit fear and despair. While it's easy to sympathize with mothers who complain their husbands don't spend time with the children, up until recently men simply weren't allowed to participate fully in the joys of parenting. Their children and wives got cheated, but so did the men. While it's easy to sympathize with women who complain their men spend their weekends and vacations working, consider what it must be like to be one of those men, unable to let go of burdens and chores and simply play and have fun. And while it's easy to sympathize with women who complain their men don't talk about personal things, consider what it must be like to be one of those men, without the permission and experience to express their innermost thoughts and feelings.

In other words, male socialization has provided little to help men in maintaining intimate relationships. Men generally don't get a great deal of understanding because they don't know how to ask for it. And depending upon the extent to which they were taught to repress their feelings, they may not even know what hurts.

A man typically won't let even a friend get close enough to know his vulnerabilities for fear he will later be run through with the damning evidence of his weakness. The risk is too great: If he lets another man see that soft spot behind the armor, he will get speared.

Any attempt to get down to that place he himself fears to know—even an attempt by you—can disturb his sense of security and make him want to hide. Watch him duck behind the newspaper, turn on the TV, or pretend he is asleep.

But you could be the one person with whom he can feel secure; you could offer him a safe place—if he can trust you enough to become vulnerable.

Smith underlines the importance of such trust. Many of the participants in Smith's workshops at Esalen have been couples where one or both partners have occupations with great power and responsibility. In short, they are captains of industry. Smith observed that often such individuals described themselves as autonomous and even armored in their worklife (because of the authority they must carry). But they have one place where they can drop their defenses and become quite vulnerable, and that is alone with their partner.

If you can build such a trust with your own partner, you can achieve greater intimacy that will, in turn, open your relationship to heightened levels of romance.

But where do you start?

Accepting His Love

In the survey for this book, more than 82 percent of male respondents rated the statement "Be supportive of my career" as important to their relationship. And nearly 90 percent rated as important "Show appreciation for what I do for her." What's most telling, however, is that men said they are not getting the appreciation they desire from their partners. Women may not realize that much of what a man does every day is done for the woman he loves.

Dr. Daphne Rose Kingma, a therapist who specializes in men's issues, addresses that concern in her book *The Men We Never Knew:*

> In the actions-that-mean-I-love-you category, most men view their financial support, in particular, to be the visible expression of their love. The mere fact that they get up every day and go to work to support their wives and children is for them the absolute proof that they love their family. That's why so many men are aggravated when the women in their lives keep saying to them, "But tell me that you love me." It feels to them as if nothing they've done means anything. They feel depressed, hopeless, and stupid because, without

consciously being aware of it, they hoped and expected that the eight to ten hours a day they spend at work every week would be saying the "I love you" and they're shocked to discover that it hasn't.

"But I get up and go to work every day, too," you may protest. Certainly women have proven that they can play the role of provider as well as that of nurturer. Today millions of women contribute financially to their households. But a woman doesn't typically see this as an expression of love; rather, it is something that she wants to do for herself or that she needs to do to support herself and possibly her family. Before the women's movement, men did not ask women to join the workforce. On the contrary: when women went to work, men got less of what they expected from their partners at home. It was women who changed the system. And in general men still regard their own activities—all those things they do around the house and for the children, as well as their daily work—to be their side of the love contribution.

According to Kingma, "Both men and women have revised what they are doing—women now work and men now change diapers—but we still haven't changed the way our collective social unconscious views our respective responsibilities. In our hearts, women are still the nurturers and men are still responsible for everything else."

Responding to the survey, men clearly stated their desire to receive recognition for what they do on a daily basis. The statement "Treat me as very important in her life" was rated highly by more than 80 percent of survey respondents. This desire also came through in the responses to the open-ended question "Has there ever been a time when a partner made you feel really special?" A few examples:

"Yes. When she shows her appreciation for me—for who I am and what I do for her."

"After I spent time fixing her bike, she came and asked what she could do for me. I certainly hadn't expected anything in return, but it showed me that she appreciated the time I spent on her things."

"When she saw that I had finished installing a ceiling fan in the bedroom that she had wanted for a long time, she smiled, clapped, and baked me some cookies."

In order to feel loved, a man does not need to hear those three little words. He needs to know that you appreciate what he does for you. One man wrote (as if to his partner), "I want you to appreciate the things I do to provide for and protect you. If these things aren't important to you, tell me what is important so I can try to adjust and provide value to you. I want to help you, so let me know how to help you."

In order to romance your sweetheart, it is critical that you let him know how much you value the role that his work plays in your relationship. You might say, for example, "I appreciate the fact that you get up every morning to spend your days working so that we can live as comfortably as we do." Or: "I appreciate the extra work you're doing now so that we can afford to help Susie through college."

Kingma underlines the need for women to show appreciation, and she suggests that we don't do it enough: "Being grateful would totally and categorically revise the chemistry of male-female relationships. For starters, it would immediately bring women down from the shabby pedestals of our passivity-oriented power, the power of the underdog, slave, and martyr, and acknowledge that men have pleased us and desire to please us. Living in the state of gratitude would open us to receive something different from men—their feelings instead of their actions."

Learn to recognize how he is showing his love. Tell him at least once a week that all those things he does—carrying in the groceries, changing the oil in your car, washing the windows, moving the couch, advising you on your next business presentation—are important to you. "Thank you for fixing the shower. I feel you love me when you make life easier for me." Give him credit for doing things that you could just as well have done for yourself. Celebrate his role in your relationship and in the family. Accept the way that your partner communicates love.

And when you give him credit for the way he shows you love, do it without any expectations for yourself. That's romance.

Activities to Hone Your Romantic Spirit

Start developing your own romantic philosophy. As you read ideas and exercises throughout this book, make honest decisions about which things you feel comfortable doing and where you must draw a line. Be honest with yourself. Use your imagination. Make it fun. Try coming up with some of your own exercises to romance the man you love.

The following are examples of actions and activities that, according to our survey respondents, express the romantic spirit. Try only those that suit your personality as well as your partner's desires.

- Ask your partner to take part in an exercise with you: Each of you writes a description of yourself as if you were writing an ad for a personals column. Describe only your good points. The one rule here is to refrain from judging what the other writes; each of you is giving intimate information about how you would like to be viewed. Encourage your partner by adding some of the characteristics that you especially appreciate about him. Note what he writes so that you can praise him in the days to come for the qualities that are important to him. This exercise will not only reveal intimate information about each of you, but it will also make you more vulnerable with each other, which is the truest road to intimacy.
- Without involving your partner, think back on all the expectations you had of him when you met. Think of the ways in which you set yourself up for disappointment. Then, in your mind, forgive your partner. And tell him out loud that you love him for how he makes you feel today.
- Begin an appreciation program. At least once a week, let your partner know how much you value his work, the chores he does around the house, and his attention to the

children—even if it is "his job" to do these things. Imagine what it would be like if he weren't there to help, and give him ample credit for making your life easier.

- If you are in the habit of greeting your partner each evening with facts about your own day, your concerns, or problems that need his attention, your greeting may signal anxiety rather than romance. Practice holding back until later in the evening to discuss such things. When you greet each other, focus on the inclusion process, the connecting process. Put that first. Your partner will be much more willing to listen to the experiences and difficulties of your day after he has had a chance to relax and accept the romance of being with you.
- Start paying attention to anything your partner says or does that may be related to his desires for romance. Write these ideas down in a private notebook. And begin planning ways to satisfy those desires.
- Based on your partner's individual preferences, think of one special thing you can do today that will both surprise and delight him.
- If you don't already have a calendar, get one, and start scribbling little reminders on it of all the ways you plan to romance your partner. Today is only the beginning.

2

Communicating His Way

There once was a woman who fell in love. She was so happy that she had finally found a man willing to share his feelings. He spoke of his past joys and disappointments as well as his future hopes and dreams.

He listened to everything she said. He hugged her when she was sad. He responded thoughtfully when she had a concern. And he told her that he loved her.

Their soulful embrace lasted for years. But one day the woman noticed that her lover no longer spoke of his feelings. He no longer listened to her daily concerns. And she realized that he hadn't said "I love you" for many months.

That wonderfully expressive man with whom she had fallen in love was lost. Where did he go?

Meeting His Communication Needs

In courtship, a man may unwittingly lead his partner to believe that she has at last found a man who can express what he feels. But after a few years, or even a few months, that same man may be talking only in terms of facts and things and objectives. When you ask him about his day, instead of expressing the excitement of finally attaining a goal, he'll say, "The offer came through." If you ask him how he feels, instead of sharing his joy or sadness, he responds in terms of his body: "I'm bushed."

What's going on?

11

Courtship is a discovery process. When two people meet, they have years and years of past to communicate to each other: facts and feelings about growing up, about careers, and maybe even about former love relationships. But once they are seeing each other on a steady basis, there are rarely any grand emotional events to discuss. And although women often desire to share their daily ups and downs, men generally want to put such things behind them in order to relax. If a woman tries to get her partner to open up, he may react by clamming up. The result is communication conflict.

According to Dr. Deborah Tannen, sociolinguist and author of *You Just Don't Understand,* when a woman talks about her desire for intimacy, a man may interpret this as an attempt to control him. Consequently, he pulls away from her, which only increases her need to be closer. Tannen writes: "Her attempts to get closer will aggravate his fear, and his reaction—pulling further away—will aggravate hers, and so on, in an ever-widening spiral. Understanding each other's styles, and the motives behind them, is a first move in breaking this destructive circuit."

Dr. Gerald Smith illustrates this point through an exercise he uses in his workshops at Esalen Institute:

> I ask each woman to stand close to her partner, up against him, physically touching him. Neither partner can move toward the other because there is no room to do so. The only way to have intimacy is the paradox—having space—so that the woman can experience the man moving toward her. If a woman is always trying to be so close to her partner—asking him how he feels, what he thinks, and so forth—the only place he can move is away from her. He feels crowded. And instead of generating intimacy, she actually generates withdrawal. Unless she gives him space, she will never feel him moving in her direction.

The importance—and challenge—of communication between the sexes surfaced in a number of ways in the results from the men's survey. First, men complained that women want them to express their feelings. "Why does she always want to know how I feel about something?" wrote one man. "I felt fine until she asked. Now I feel tired." Another wrote:

"When I do express my feelings, we get into an argument—whatever I say either makes her angry or makes her cry."

Furthermore, there is frustration with what some men call "overcommunication": "What's wrong with just being together, in the quiet? Why do women have this need to fill every void with mundane chatter?"

Some men are disappointed in the reaction to their attempts to communicate: "She's always asking me about what I like and what I want, but when I tell her, she starts complaining about all she's not getting. I can't win!"

And there were at least a few comments about expectations: "If I hear once more, 'If you loved me, you would . . . ,' I'll crack up. What does she think I am, a mind reader? How should I know what she wants? Whenever I ask, she gets coy and doesn't tell me."

Why is communication between the sexes so complicated? You would think that if two people love each other, they would be able to communicate just fine.

Not so, according to Tannen. Her studies found that communication between men and women is cross-cultural: each sex has its own conversational style. Instead of different dialects, men and women have their own "genderlects." Moreover, they talk for different reasons. While women communicate to gain intimacy, men communicate to gain status. For women, then, home is the most natural place for communication; but for men, communication at home isn't necessary.

As Tannen explains: "For everyone, home is a place to be off-stage. But the comfort of home can have opposite and incompatible meanings for women and men. For many men, the comfort of home means freedom from having to prove themselves and impress through verbal display. At last, they are in a situation where talk is not required. They are free to remain silent. But for women, home is a place where they are free to talk, and where they feel the greatest need for talk, with those they are closest to."

The way the women's movement has changed society is forcing men to express themselves more. But as men get closer

to the "female" way of communicating, it would be appropriate for women to accept and acknowledge the "male" way of
communicating.

There are, of course, many men roaming the earth who communicate their desires and emotions at least as well as their
partners do, and your sweetheart may be one of them. But
whatever the case, as one survey respondent wrote: "There can
be no communication without goodwill. A woman won't understand you unless she wants to."

Respect His Quiet Zone

Men seem overwhelmed by women's talk. Again and again, the
men's survey brought up the need for "peace and quiet." Here
are a few examples:

"I arrive home first, and everything is quiet. I like that. I wish that
when my partner arrived we could share that quiet, just relaxing
together. But she always wants to talk, and usually it's about things
that are very mundane and, frankly, boring to me. I go through a
lot of boring things during the day as well, but what's the point of
going through it all again? Let's forget about the day and just share
our time together."

"With my first wife, I always got a line of grief every night I walked
into the house. My coping mechanism was to come home later and
later. Pretty soon I didn't come home at all."

"I have been married and divorced twice, and I've been in about twenty
other relationships with women that might have come to something.
But what always made me run was the tedious talk-talk-talk every
woman had to go through every night. I didn't want to hear it."

"My wife is from a large, vociferous family. She loves to talk.
Every evening she has to tell me the simplest details of her day.
In the first few years of marriage, I cringed just walking in the
door. Her talking often sounded like a complaint, and it made
me feel as if it were my fault. I couldn't figure out what I did
wrong or what she wanted me to do. But I came to realize that
she only needed me to listen. And after a tussle or two, I also

realized how important this was for her. And it didn't take much on my part, just to listen. After twenty years of marriage and a house full of kids, I think that just listening to her for a bit every evening has helped keep our marriage happy."

In each of these cases, the woman did not intend to make the man uncomfortable. No one was right or wrong, but if a woman realizes that she may be affecting her partner in a negative way, she will at least be prepared to accept his response.

If a man doesn't want to interact at the end of the workday, his partner may think that he is avoiding her, he doesn't want to be with her, or maybe he doesn't even love her. But that's just not so. He *does* want to share with her: he wants to share his happy peacefulness, which is what he believes he has earned. This is the best of his day—the best of his life—and he longs to share it with the woman he loves.

As one survey respondent wrote: "I like being together with my partner without interacting—reading, walking, watching TV. I like to feel her next to me."

Men yearn to spend quiet times just being with their partner, doing whatever it is either of them wants to do, speaking only when there is something relevant to be shared. Men enjoy the connection that comes without conversation.

In the end, communication styles may require some negotiation. If you want to hold your partner's attention (as well as his good feelings about being with you), you may do well to limit your talk about your day to those things that would actually interest him. He may have the same sort of fleeting thoughts that you express to him, but he doesn't think they are important enough to vocalize; therefore he dismisses them, as he may very well dismiss yours. Limiting your conversation will benefit you as well as him, because if you tend to chatter about topics or incidents that don't interest him, he will stop listening.

Because of men's tendency to stop listening, some women have adopted a strategy of ending each sentence with a question that demands a response, such as "Do you see what I mean?" or "Right?" or "Don't you think so?" Or they may begin their monologues with "Tell me what you think of this." Unfortunately, such strategies usually irritate men and, in some cases, drive them to another space where they won't be bothered—sometimes away from home.

An alternative is for you and your partner to agree to set aside a special time for discussing what's going on in your lives. This special time will be for talking about difficulties, concerns, and the relationship. If you want to make this work, it is critical that you adhere to the schedule—maybe it's a half an hour each evening, maybe it's a few hours every Sunday afternoon. You can do this at home (if you are assured of no interruptions), or you can do it while pursuing an activity together, such as an evening walk or a Sunday brunch. But it's important that the two of you are alone and that each gives the other equal listening and talking time. Again, this is to take the place of the regular evening discussion; so unless you cut back on that, you won't be able to interest your partner in keeping up the scheduled talk time.

"But that's not enough," you might say. "I need to share so much more." If this is the case, try increasing your time with women friends. A good friend will probably be more solicitous than your partner could be. Growing up, girls learn intimacy early on, and they learn to support each other's feelings. Instead of trying to fix things, they feel comfortable just hugging their friends or saying, "Aw, I'm sorry you don't feel well," or they may encourage more talk with, "And then what happened?" Women friends generally offer each other more comfort and support than most men know how to provide. Arrange more time with your friends when you can talk about your daily trials and tribulations; set up a regular luncheon, meet for an occasional hour after work, or call friends to talk on the phone a few times a week.

Let your partner know what you're up to. Tell him that you need to spend more time with friends so that you don't burden him with what he might consider your "emotional baggage."

If these arrangements don't work, you might try following the equal-time rule—not equal speaking time, but equal "being" time. One survey respondent told of how he and his wife resolved this dilemma: "My wife has accepted my need for quiet as I have accepted her need for sharing. I tell her, 'I will give you full attention for an hour and listen to whatever you want to say if you will then spend an hour with me in complete silence.' It's been our salvation. And our relationship has continued for all these years."

Some couples even have ways of signaling a need for quiet. If a man does not feel like communicating, he will put on a cap or visor. This signals that he wants a recess, he needs to withdraw. Of course, such an arrangement has to be worked out in advance so that the woman doesn't feel personally slighted.

If you explore options with your partner and negotiate styles, you will find him paying more attention to the important things you have to communicate.

Listen to His Ideas

In spite of the fact that many men may be less than articulate about their feelings, they do have ideas that they want to share with their partners. But it seems that no one is listening. "Listen to my ideas" was the highest rated statement on the survey. Nearly 100 percent of male survey respondents rated it as important to their relationship.

So why aren't women listening?

"Let's face it," said one woman queried about this issue. "Man talk can be really boring. It's all lecturing and explaining and details about a thing or a game or an activity. It has nothing to do with them or me or life. I really don't care to know all the details of his favorite team's latest plays or the inner workings of his computer or the history of the company down the street from where he works. It's just not relevant to our lives or our relationship."

Tannen offers perspective: "Men's interest in the details of politics, news, and sports is parallel to women's interest in the details of personal lives. . . . And exchanging details about public news rather than private news has the advantage that it does not make men personally vulnerable: The information they are bartering has nothing to do with them."

If your partner speaks of seemingly mundane things, don't shut him off. This may be the way that he initiates conversation with you. These are not throwaway lines; they are openings. If you put him off, he may never get to what's important. Your partner's ideas are critical to him, and he wants you to value them. Remember when you were courting and you asked him about his ideas? Just as you now wonder what ever happened to his interest in feelings, he wonders what happened to your curiosity about his thoughts.

Start listening again, and he just may begin to value conversation with you the way he once did.

Be There for Him

Most women have extensive networks of emotional support. They can generally turn to neighbors, professional associates, old school chums, sisters, mothers. Women are capable of letting down their defenses and becoming vulnerable with each other.

But where do men go for emotional support?

What men talk about in their locker rooms suggests they don't go to one another, for the conversation there is vastly different from conversation in women's locker rooms. While women may share secrets about their children, relationships, or even professional insecurities, men generally do not show vulnerability or disclose weaknesses. Instead, they banter, joke, and thus protect themselves. For a man, discussing a personal problem reveals a weakness. If he has a problem, he will most likely relate it in factual terms—and often only after he has solved it.

Because women are the traditional nurturers, a man usually looks to a woman to provide emotional support. And if the man is your partner, you want that woman to be you.

In his 1969 novel *Mr. Bridge,* Evan S. Connell wrote from the point of view of a husband and father. What his protagonist thought, as well as what he chose to express, illuminates the male inner dilemma. The novel is written from the point of view of Mr. Bridge:

> Often he thought: My life did not begin until I knew her.
>
> She would like to hear this, he was sure, but he did not know how to tell her. In the extremity of passion he cried out in a frantic voice: "I love you!" yet even these words were unsatisfactory. He wished for something else to say. He needed to let her know how deeply he felt her presence while they were lying together during the night, as well as each morning when they awoke and in the evening when he came home. However, he could think of nothing appropriate.
>
> So the years passed, they had three children and accustomed themselves to a life together, and eventually Mr. Bridge decided that his wife should expect nothing more of him. After all, he was an attorney rather than a poet; he could never pretend to be what he was not.

Connell's novel portrays a man who longs for greater intimacy, who longs to show his deep love toward wife and family, but who instead shows only restraint. The expression of his love continually eludes him.

Though Mr. and Mrs. Bridge have a particularly provincial lifestyle that may be very different from your own, this male longing is not unusual. Just knowing that your own partner may be longing desperately for a closer relationship with you—a longing that he is at a loss to express—should encourage you not only to accept what he offers but also to help him open up his feelings to you and others around him. This requires a great deal of acceptance as well as restraint on your part. Consider a few sad examples from the men's survey that show how easily a woman can shut down a man's attempt at openness:

> "I was in a mixed group one evening when several women began complaining about men not expressing feelings. They went on and on until one man said: 'Okay, but what if the man cries?' And one of the women responded, 'But a man isn't supposed to cry!' "

> "Many years ago when I was beginning my career, the company I was with went through a down period. People were laid off, and I was told I might be demoted from my newly acquired supervisory job. I went home very upset and told my wife about it and

expressed my dismay. She thought I was weak for reacting the way I did, and I resolved never to reveal myself in that way again."

"Any woman who really wants her man to express his feelings had better be prepared for the full range of emotions—not just 'I love you!' "

Nearly 90 percent of male survey respondents rated the statement "Listen to my concerns" as important to the relationship. And more than 75 percent highly rated "Empathize with my feelings." But how can you listen if he doesn't talk?

If your partner isn't opening up to you, try to establish an environment of greater trust. A partner who feels safe being close to you—which means no expectations and no judgments on your part—may eventually feel safe enough to ask for your emotional support.

Fortunately, increasing numbers of men seem to be getting in touch with their feelings and even expressing those feelings. Witness the ordeal of U.S. Air Force Captain Scott O'Grady when he was shot down over Bosnia in the summer of '95. For six days he hid from enemy patrols in the woods, mostly face-down in the dirt, eating grass and ants, and drinking rainwater wrung from his socks. He was a well-trained, well-disciplined pilot. And yet, once he was back in safe territory, he was able to shed tears and confess that he was no Rambo. "Nah, I'm not a hero," he said. "All I was was a scared little bunny rabbit trying to hide, trying to survive."

Hopefully your own partner won't have to undergo such an ordeal to become open to his emotions. With your help, he can reach safe territory right here at home. And once he feels safe with you, the intimacy of your relationship knows no bounds.

If your partner doesn't express feelings easily, support him in getting in touch with his emotions by helping him connect specific emotional reactions to incidents he reports to you. This will help him to perceive that he *does* feel things. Instead of hearing only the words that he says, listen to the spaces in between. His emotions may show up in his facial expressions, in his gestures, in his stance.

When he tells you about something that he seems to think is significant, ask him how he felt about it. Ask him what it meant for him to experience it. Without prying, ask not only for details about the event but also for his responses. This will help him start to express his feelings to you.

If he mentions something that happened at work—"they moved my office"—you can ask him how he feels in his new office. Does he like it better? What caused the move—a reward for a job well done or company politics?

Maybe he witnessed something on the way home from work: "I saw a deer killed along the highway." Ask him how he felt. Was he sad? Was he afraid that a deer might jump in front of his car? Was he angry that someone was driving too fast?

His relationship with his children may elicit some of his strongest emotions. When a son or daughter is hurt, receives an honor or a demerit, or simply asks Dad for help, seek out your partner's response—pride, disappointment, fear, anger, hope, satisfaction, or maybe a range of emotions. Do his children evoke his past—the joys and sorrows of growing up? What was that like?

One way to draw out his feelings is to offer your own: "I'm so proud when I see Jessie up there playing in the band." Or: "It makes me sad to think how vulnerable those innocent deer are to highway traffic."

If you want to know what's going on inside your partner, instead of asking him, disclose some of what you are feeling. It's difficult, for example, to respond to the question, "Why don't you tell me what you're feeling?" Instead, to open up the path to disclosure, you might say, "I'm feeling out of touch right now," or "I'm feeling confused. I'm not sure what's going on with you." As a physical parallel, imagine a game of strip poker: Your partner will be much more comfortable taking off some of his clothes if he knows you are willing to do the same.

It's important not to badger him with questions every day (that's communicating *your* way). Take it slowly. Eventually he may become more in touch with his feelings—or at least learn how to express them more clearly. Watch to see whether this process is comfortable for him. If certain feelings are too painful for expression, he may want to forget about them for now. If that's the case, don't push it. Just let him be.

When he is ready to open his heart, you must not judge or criticize. Hold your tongue and listen. We all have a right to our own feelings. So don't tell your partner what he should or shouldn't feel. If you start to judge, he'll pull right back into his shell, and then you may have lost forever your chances for greater intimacy. Instead, build his trust in you. Let him know that he will be safe confiding in the woman he loves.

This is one place, however, where you don't want to set any goals. A woman makes a mistake when she sets a goal of getting her partner to disclose his feelings more often or to a certain depth. As she works to achieve this goal, her partner feels cornered: he believes that he will never measure up, that he will never be able to do this well enough. Don't focus on the extent to which your partner can reveal himself. What really matters is the direction—whether he is becoming more open over time.

Viewing disclosure in this way will help you let go of the need to know how he feels at any given moment. Instead of quickly moving in when you sense he is upset, for example, try inviting your partner to open up when he feels comfortable. You might say, "When you feel like it, I'd be glad to talk with you about this," or "When it feels comfortable for you, let me know; I'd like to spend some time on this." In other words, give him an invitation to talk about his feelings that clearly shows your concern but that also allows him room to express the feelings on his terms. This message shows support but does not crowd.

Not all men, however, will accept the invitation. In spite of all your attempts to help, your partner may be unready or unwilling to express his emotions. In the spaces between his words are hopes and fears that he may not recognize or that he may not want to acknowledge, even to himself. Listening means listening with your whole self to everything your partner is saying as well as to what he isn't saying. But remember that some part of each of us is a dark forest, where no one can follow.

Activities to Hone Your Romantic Spirit

- Practice quiet. Do this in a way that won't make your partner think you are angry with him. For one week, greet him in a loving way each evening. Ask him about his day, say something brief about your day, and then get on with whatever you need to do and let him alone. When the week is up, tell him what you've been up to, and ask him whether he has been enjoying his peace and quiet.
- While your partner is relaxing, perhaps reading or watching TV, in a common room (not in his own room or office), go sit near him without saying a word. Work on your own project, read your book, watch the show. If you feel the urge to talk, go to another room and call a friend or relative. Or write your partner a love letter.
- If you don't already practice meditation, take a class to learn how to do it. Try meditating when your partner wants quiet time alone.
- Invite your partner for a walk in the moonlight. Say nothing. If he speaks, comment on the topic he has chosen. Do not bring up any subjects on your own.
- If you need more listening time from your partner, ask him whether he would set aside a limited amount of time each week or even each day to discuss what's going on in your lives. Stick to the schedule.
- Set up an equal-time schedule. You get to air your feelings and solicit his for a certain period of time, and then he gets to share an equal period of time with you, doing what he wants to do.
- If you are in the habit of trying to change your partner so that he will communicate as you do, contemplate the social

and parental forces that shaped him—his "male" training—
and try to accept *his* communication style.

- The next time your partner relates an event of signifi-
cance, try to elicit his feelings about it. Ask him if he felt
proud, fearful, anxious, or whatever you believe the feeling to be, based upon your reading between the lines. If
he is unwilling or unable to respond, don't force it.
- The next time your child does something significant,
relate the news to your partner in terms of your own
feelings: "I'm so proud of Jeremy for getting the scholar-
ship." "I'm so relieved that Melissa got on the team."
"I'm worried about Joshua's math scores." See whether
your partner picks up on the *feeling* part of the message.
If you think it's appropriate, ask him about his feelings
on the subject.
- If your partner chooses to open up to you, help him feel
emotionally safe. Practice keeping your responses to
yourself when he presents feelings that you find inappro-
priate or irrelevant. After all, they are his feelings, and
they are no less valid than yours. Consciously listen without judging. Try not to interpret his thoughts and feelings
as a reflection on you.

Getting What You Need

A man generally considers his love relationship to be happy if
his partner is happy. Despite all the talking his partner might
do, however, the man is often frustrated that she doesn't communicate what she really wants. She talks about how she
feels—including her disappointment in not getting what she
wants—but she doesn't clearly state what that is.

Be Clear About Your Purpose

In recounting her daily problems and concerns, a woman can
confuse her partner, leading him to believe that he has done

something wrong when, in fact, she may simply need a little sympathy from him.

In *Men Are from Mars, Women Are from Venus,* Dr. John Gray writes, "When women talk about problems, men usually resist. A man assumes she is talking with him about her problems because she is holding him responsible. The more problems, the more he feels blamed. He does not realize that she is talking to feel better. A man doesn't know that she will appreciate it if he just listens."

A man may respond by trying to solve his partner's problems. She may then feel that he is belittling the problems. "If your job is so bad," he might say, "then quit." That's not what she needs to hear. To make matters worse, if she doesn't accept his solutions, he feels rejected.

In another scenario, if he thinks she is blaming him, he may feel attacked and become defensive, arguing with her.

When you have concerns to relate, let your partner know in advance what you need from him. Maybe you do want his opinion or maybe you do need his help, but if you only want him to listen, tell him that. Let him know that you need his emotional support or understanding of your situation and nothing more. Tell him that you need to feel that he cares about you on a daily basis. And if all you want is a hug, say so. If you make your needs very clear, he'll be much more willing to listen to your words—and your feelings.

Ask for What You Want

Ask for something? But Mother taught me that asking isn't polite. Accept what is offered—that's what I should do.

Because women are taught not to ask, when they finally do, their request is often expressed in terms of hurt, guilt, or resentment.

"Why doesn't she just tell me what she wants?" wrote one frustrated man who responded to the survey. "Then I could do it and we'd be happy. She likes surprises. But if I don't come through, I'm in the doghouse for a week."

Maybe you're a better communicator than this man's partner, but take a look at the following statements. Do any of these sound familiar?

"He knows I don't like iceberg lettuce, but that's all he ever gets."

"He leaves me every Thursday evening for his time with the guys. There's so much here to do. Is he blind?"

"I hinted about that little bracelet I wanted for my birthday. But he had to get me the bread maker, which was three times as expensive. He just doesn't get it."

"He never tells me he loves me anymore. I guess he doesn't care."

"He doesn't write or call when he goes away on business trips. He must have another woman with him."

"I keep talking about the rose garden that Julia's husband planted for her, but would George ever do that for me? I bet it's never even entered his mind."

"He knows I'd love to go to New Orleans, but when he went there last month on a business trip, did he ask me to go?"

Is it fair to expect our partners to know what we want, and then accuse them of failing us when they don't provide it? More than a few survey respondents had something to say about this. One example, from a divorced man: "If only she had let me know what she wanted from me, I believe we would still be together."

But before you run off to present your partner with a list, think about him as your audience. When a particular style of communication isn't working, a person will frequently try that same style even harder. It's like shouting at someone who cannot understand your language. How have you communicated your desires in the past? If your partner hasn't gotten your message, it's time to try a new way of communicating. When is he most receptive? What is the best manner in which to approach him? What can you do to get his attention without annoying him? What is the best way to present your needs?

You might try inviting your partner on a walk or out to lunch. Get away from daily interruptions and reminders of household chores. It's important that you let him know what's bothering you, what you want that you aren't getting, and what would give you joy. Try to elicit the same from him.

The key to success may lie in your approach: Present your point of view, then ask for his. Rather than beginning with "Why don't you . . . ," say, "I would enjoy it if you would. . . ." Rather than saying, "Don't you know that . . . ," explain to him, "I believe that . . ." or "I feel that. . . ." If you keep your problem on your side of the fence, your partner will be much less inclined to be defensive about it—and much more inclined to try to help solve it.

Of course, the expression of need doesn't guarantee its satisfaction, but you can bet that your partner will do his best to fulfill your wishes if he can.

Any area of your relationship that you feel could be improved might be a topic for your discussion. Some examples:

- How you spend your time: Would you like more time with your partner, more family time with the children, more time alone, more time with friends? Let him know. How would you prefer to spend your time with your partner? How would he prefer to spend time with you?
- What each of you contributes toward household maintenance: Would you appreciate more of his help? Do you need outside help? Can he help you get the children to participate regularly in chores?
- What you would like your partner to do or say to help you feel sexier: Are there old demons lurking between the sheets? How can your partner help to expel them so that you can better enjoy lovemaking?
- Which gifts are important: Though this may seem trivial, men appreciate having a clear idea about what to give their partner. You don't have to point out a particular gift; just letting him know the sorts of things you would enjoy receiving (a romantic dinner, a piece of jewelry, his help on a project) will help him learn how to please you. Some women fill in important dates on their partners' calendars

so that the men don't face embarrassment on anniversaries or birthdays.

- What has upset you lately: Be sure to describe the incident in terms of your feelings ("I felt hurt when you . . .").

It is critical that this discussion does not leave your partner feeling guilty, embarrassed, humiliated, or unloved. If you want to let him know about a behavior that is particularly troubling, speak of it in terms of how it affects you rather than in terms of his personality (instead of "You're an irresponsible person," try "I feel angry when you come home late"). Be as positive as you can. Interject comments about the wonderful things he does to make you feel loved.

Furthermore, if this kind of discussion is new to you, don't expect your partner to spin on a dime and say, "Yes, of course." He may need to spend a little time taking everything in. Take it slowly. Be patient. This is for the long term.

If you receive what you want from your relationship, you will be much more willing to give your partner what he wants. If your partner knows what you want, he will try to please you. And he will be pleased that you are happy. And that's romantic.

Activities to Hone Your Romantic Spirit

- The next time your partner appears worried, afraid, or anxious, simply hold his hand or hug him and tell him that you love him. If he shows signs of wanting to be left alone, let him be and occupy yourself with something else.
- When you have feelings to relate to your partner, let him know ahead of time what you would like from him in response. Approach the talk with a stated objective (I need support, I need a decision, I need your help, I need you to listen, I need a hug). If he attempts to solve your problems or becomes defensive, remind him that you need him only to listen and understand.

- Think of the phrase "If he loved me, he would . . ." and visualize all the things you have expected him to deliver as part of your romance. Now focus on those that are realistic. Choose a time and place where he is likely to be receptive to conversation. And whatever you say, be sure to speak in terms of "I" rather than "you." He isn't at fault for not delivering what he can't possibly know you want.
- Start asking for what you want on a regular basis. Be polite. Don't wait until you are frustrated or angry about your needs not being met. If you haven't gotten what you wanted in the past, think back on how you asked for it. Asking for something doesn't guarantee its arrival, but the more seriously you approach the asking, the more likely you are to get it—or at least to get an explanation of why this desire won't be fulfilled.
- When you have a complaint, explain your feelings to your partner rather than dwelling on what your partner did (or didn't do) to upset you.

3

Taking Time . . . Spending Time

When two people fall in love, they strive to spend lots of time together. They carve out special time from their schedules to be alone with each other. Time together flies by so quickly that even as they part, they are anxious to see each other again. But once they enter a long-term relationship, their time together soon fills with the mundane demands of everyday life.

Thus, it isn't surprising that more than 75 percent of the men surveyed rated "romantic evenings together (in or out)" and "romantic weekends together (home or away)" as important to their love relationship. Special time alone with your partner can bring back some of those wonderful romantic feelings that are all too often swept off in the wake of fast-moving life. In order to make it happen, however, you need to make it a priority. But if you do, it will certainly pay off.

Romantic evenings and weekends take a little extra planning (especially if you have children), but if you and your partner create special times to focus on each other, you just may find some new excitement to share.

Creating Special Time at Home

What interferes with romance? Men's answers to this open-ended survey question were both specific and consistent. The bottom line? Everyday living. Here are some examples:

"Business commitments, stress, preoccupations."

31

"Life, jobs, kids, responsibilities."

"Duties, chores, and things that break."

"Social obligations, interruptions, irrelevant distractions."

"Phone, TV, neighbors, friends, and relatives."

"Lack of time. Being tired. Being too busy for even the minor touching."

"Children and work, financial limitations, and overexpectations when we do get away."

Although you can't rid your relationship of such consuming distractions, you can create small interludes that offer romantic respite.

Create Space Pockets

A man longs for a happy home to which he can return at the end of the day. In fact, the desire for a peaceful home life was a recurrent theme in survey responses, particularly from men who share a home with the woman they love:

> "Whenever I arrive home or she arrives home, she always comes up to me and smiles and says, 'Where's my kiss?' It's kinda cute and corny, but it shows me that she's glad to see me and she wants to connect."

> "When my wife greets me with a happy smile, I'm glad to be home and I want to spend time with her."

> "I come home from a business trip, or even from my office any day of the week, where I have had lots of women catering to me—my secretary, the flight attendant, the women (as well as men) who report to me—but I only want to be with my own sweet partner. It is so pleasurable to find her happy to see me. If the house is peaceful and she has taken special care to greet me with a smile and maybe even groomed herself to look especially inviting, I feel so grateful to be coming home to her. I understand that she has a lot of concerns to deal with during her day, but when I arrive home, I need to know that I please her. And that's what she shows me when she tries to please me."

The after-work greeting is key. Whether you arrive home first or your partner does, the greeting is an opportunity to take a few minutes out of whatever you're doing to show him—with warmth and appreciation—how pleased you are that he's there for you. Whether it's a simple "Hi honey" or a big hug and kiss, focusing on him at this time will start the evening on a romantic note. Even if you've got a crying baby in your arms or little Joey is tugging at Daddy's hand, your look, your kiss, your words of affection will show your partner that he pleases you.

According to survey respondents, the way a man spends time with his partner is critical to the romantic quality of the relationship. The greeting is a great beginning. But what else for him constitutes "quality time"? A few examples from the survey:

"Our mornings together are great. We wake early enough so that we don't have to rush. Sometimes we have sex, sometimes we don't. We talk. Our morning talk is the best. That's where we keep current on each other's concerns, desires, fears, dreams, or whatever. We both know how to listen without judging. One or the other of us goes downstairs to get the coffee. Sometimes one of us will bring a surprise for breakfast—a scone, a croissant, a muffin—that we sneaked in the night before. On weekend mornings, one of us will stay in the kitchen a bit longer than usual, making pancakes or eggs. If we have allowed enough time, it's terrific."

"We sit together and gaze. We don't have to speak. We breathe deeply. Sometimes we do this for 15 minutes, sometimes for an hour. It intensifies the feeling of the heart."

"Just being next to each other is a gentle, romantic way to live. I like to be in a quiet space with my partner. After the kids are in bed, we spend evenings together, nothing of importance said, occasionally calling attention to something interesting. Each of us doing whatever he or she enjoys. I usually fiddle with one of my model airplanes. She has work projects, but sometimes she plays the piano. One or the other of us does the dishes. Evenings like this are so relaxing. I enjoy this time with her."

"We meditate together. I don't know if you can characterize that as romantic, but it helps to strengthen our relationship."

But who has the time for quiet, unhurried romance? There are so many household chores to do—laundry, dishes, bills, cleaning—and they often must be done in the evening. Think about your priorities. There will always be chores to do. So give yourself, and your relationship, a break. If you and your partner can plan your chore schedules so that you have just one free evening a week to spend quietly together at home, you will quickly enhance the romantic intimacy of your relationship.

Sharing quiet time together can, of course, be difficult if you have small children in the home. They need your time, too. Yet you must protect your love relationship so that after the little birds have flown the nest, you and your partner still recognize each other. Depending on the ages of your children, you can plan romantic times when they are out with friends or after they've gone to sleep. You might consider sharing child care with a neighbor or with the parents of one of your children's friends—you take their kids every Tuesday, and they take yours every Thursday.

If romance is important to you, you can find a way.

Romance Him with Food

Eating is such a sensual pleasure that even the everyday meal— the preparing, the serving, the sharing—presents a terrific opportunity for romance.

Nearly half the men surveyed rated "Cook enjoyable meals on a regular basis" as desirable in their love relationships (the rating was higher for married men). This doesn't mean that your partner wants you to be the kitchen slave. But if you have any talent in this area, you can earn lots of romance points here.

If you enjoy cooking, discover what dishes your partner enjoys, and try to maintain some of his favorites in your repertoire. Then, every once in a while, try something new and special to delight him when he least expects it.

If he's the better chef or holds responsibility for the household cooking, you can still learn to prepare something special for him, even if it's a simple dish. Adding your own special touch—a tasty salad or dessert, for example—to a meal that he prepares may be all that's needed. And if you and your partner enjoy working together in the kitchen, you've got the recipe for romance.

Quotes from survey respondents underlined the romantic value of sharing a meal. A few examples:

> "What's romantic? When my wife goes out of the way to make a special dinner for me."

> "Dinner is a ritual, a meeting place. Sometimes we cook together, sometimes one or the other of us cooks. We talk about things that matter to both of us."

> "We cook for each other. We serve each other. We treat each other. And in that sharing is romance."

If your cooking skills are less than presentable, there are other ways to provide a meal your partner is sure to appreciate. Maybe you have a neighbor who is a great cook; barter something with him or her (baby-sitting, computer training, gardening, pet care, chauffeuring, consulting) for a gourmet meal for two. Check out the restaurant options: increasing numbers of good restaurants will prepare a meal for you to pick up; others will deliver.

When you are planning to be away from your partner at dinnertime, make something special in advance and leave it in the refrigerator for him to find. He might also appreciate a special little treat once in a while—an ice-cream bar, his favorite fruit, or even a special cookie.

Make Evening Time Meaningful

If you and your partner spend most of your evenings together watching TV (no matter what's on) and then drag yourselves like zombies to bed, it's time to introduce some new activities.

Interacting with your partner on a regular basis will not only help you keep current on each other's wants, needs, desires, and feelings, but it will also stimulate conversation and bring fun to your relationship. New interests and activities will perk up other aspects of your life as well. So help your partner get up off his duff (or is it you who needs the nudge?) and start to play.

Spending even one evening a week on something other than TV will bring a new spark to your relationship. Depending on the ages and interests of any children living at home, you may want to get them involved as well. You and your family will have your own preferences, but here are a few ideas to get you started:

- Play a game. That's what people used to do before there was TV—chess, checkers, Scrabble, gin rummy. There are also lots of new board games, which you should be able to find at your local toy store or department store. You might even start a long-running game like Monopoly, or a jigsaw puzzle, and keep it going for weeks.
- Practice yoga. You can learn basic yoga positions through books, tapes, or classes, and then practice together on a regular basis.
- Take a walk. An evening walk can be very romantic—in any kind of weather.
- Work together on the crossword puzzle in the newspaper. If you want a real challenge, try the crossword puzzle in the Sunday New York Times.
- Take a class together at your local community center or community college. If you and your partner don't mind going out during the week, pick up a class catalog and discuss what options you might both enjoy—ballroom dancing, healthful cooking, oil painting, tennis, auto repair. The choices are numerous and varied.
- Start a project in which you both can participate. Redecorate or remodel a room, for example. It might involve taking a class in sponge painting techniques or wallpaper hanging, but that can be fun in itself. Some classes may be available on videotape from your local library or paint supply store.

- Read. You can each read your own book, magazine, or newspaper; or you can share, reading to each other from a book you both enjoy. (You may be surprised at the discussions that this sort of sharing provokes.) If you have children, invite them to participate.
- Learn a language together. Buy a language program on tape and start communicating in a whole new vocabulary. You will have fun putting your new skills to work in front of others—as well as when you're alone.
- Dance in the living room to music that you both enjoy.
- Start your own film class. Pick up a book that analyzes classic films and each week choose a film to read about, and then rent the film from your local video store or library. In time you'll find that you're able to critique, interpret, and appreciate movies on a whole new level. Moreover, you and your partner will have lots to discuss.

Flirt

Some say that the basic male instinct is to hunt, and that when the chase is over, the romance is gone. In truth, there's generally not much mystery left between two people who have been in a relationship for a long time. But if you know how, you can create new intrigue. One way is by flirting.

More than 75 percent of men (85 percent of married men) rated "I would appreciate it if my partner would flirt with me" as important. And more than 80 percent of men in general (85 percent of men with children living at home) rated as important: "I would appreciate it if my partner would act playful when we are alone."

Romance is more fun when it's just a little naughty. And flirting helps create that naughty mood. If you are not accustomed to flirting, you're in for a real treat. Because this bit of fun can change your relationship dramatically.

In flirting, attitude is everything. Smile to yourself. Give your partner a wink. Picture yourself as Marlene Dietrich or

Sandra Bullock or the sexiest woman you want to be, and your partner as that elusive man you've been after for so long. Here he comes, so imagine that you've got about three minutes to win him over before he's off to dance with someone else.

Start with eye contact. And smile as you make the connection. Use his name, or better yet, a pet name.

Give him a double take from across the room: a quick glance his way, then a glance away, and then a real slow comeback, as though you want to return to something you almost missed. Smile your sexiest, slyest, most sensuous smile as you capture him with that last slow look.

Whisper in his ear. Even mundane statements take on romantic connotations if whispered: "Are you ready . . . for dinner?" "I want a bite of your chicken." "I folded your shorts."

Whispering implies a special intimacy. When whispered, even "Thanks for taking out the garbage" can sound pretty sexy. And a kiss on the neck, a tongue in the ear, or a slow sweep of your fingers through his hair adds flair.

Wear clothing that's just a bit more daring than your usual, and move toward him with your best flirting smile. Hold his gaze slightly longer than he might expect. Back off quickly, suddenly preoccupied. Then come back slowly, smiling, whispering, touching. Wow! He'll be waiting for more. This can all happen within a few minutes, or it can happen within a few hours—flirt with him when you arrive home, then go change your clothes or start up the stove or open the mail, and come back to him with that great flirting style.

More than a few men wrote of their romantic fantasy to start over again with their present partner so that they could experience all those wonderful feelings that accompany meeting and courtship. Flirting can give you that new beginning. The key is trust.

If flirting is new to your relationship, your partner may not be ready to respond as you would like just yet. Flirting requires patience, subtlety, and confidence. Keep it up, and he'll be playing along soon enough.

With mutual trust, such play allows men to drop their defenses, and it allows women to take more risks. Your partner may find you as exciting as a new woman in his life, but he'll be doubly pleased because he doesn't want a new woman, just new excitement—from you.

Date at Home

Remember all the fun you used to have just necking on the couch? Well, even if that old couch is long gone, with a little planning, you can bring back romance at home.

If you want to plan something special, let your partner know ahead of time so that he'll be in the mood when he arrives. Send him an invitation, if you like, or merely hint that you'll be waiting for him tonight.

A romantic evening at home requires the right atmosphere. First of all, you've got to be alone. This may mean that the baby is asleep or that the kids are spending the night at their friends' houses. Be sure to give yourself plenty of time before your partner arrives, to relax by yourself and focus on the evening ahead, so that *you'll* be ready when he is.

Take charge of the atmosphere. Low light, music that you both enjoy, and a comfy place to snuggle add to the effect. Bring pillows to the couch and food and drink to the living room table. Turn off the TV. Turn off the ringer on the phone. Invite him to sit with you and cuddle. Create your own intimacy free from distraction.

A good meal can be a wonderfully romantic focus for the evening. Take the initiative. But don't get yourself into a stew over the preparation. If you can't cook something he likes without a fuss, order a meal to be brought to your home, or pick something up from a good take-out restaurant. If your partner is the chef, bring home the groceries for one of his favorite meals and help him out in the kitchen. Make it a light meal so that neither of you will be too full or groggy for what might follow. If your partner enjoys wine or beer with dinner, have his favorite label on hand. If there's a dessert, you might want to save it for later.

During dinner, pay attention to whatever he has to say. Don't talk about your concerns or problems. If he wants to discuss problems, just listen, then try to redirect the conversation to a more romantic topic—food, music, touching, sensual things.

A romantic evening doesn't have to include sex. But if you think it will, remember that some men prefer sex before eating, and some would rather eat first. Plan around your partner's preference as well as your own. For example, if you both prefer sex before dinner, chop and mix everything ahead of time so that you can quickly do the cooking afterward, either by yourself or as a team. The best menus in this case include dishes that need only a short period on the stove or in the oven as well as precooked meals that just need to be warmed up.

You can cue your partner for sex by flirting, by wearing something especially enticing, and by increasing the touching and cuddling. If he likes perfume on you, wear his favorite. Turn down the lights and turn up the heat. Be inventive and exciting. He's sure to give you his complete attention.

And after the lovemaking? A walk in the moonlight is nice.

Meet at Midday

If one or both of you works, you probably don't see each other during the day. But most workers, whether they own the building or clean the building, take time off for lunch. So how about inviting your partner to lunch?

If he says he eats while he works, tell him that you're worried about his health, that he needs to get away from his job concerns and focus on the larger picture. Depending on your physical proximity to each other at midday, you can arrange lunch at a restaurant, you can pack (or pick up) a picnic for the park, or you can meet at home (just make sure that you'll be alone). You and/or your partner might have to take some extra time off work in order to get together without rushing, but this connection will be worth it.

When you meet, greet him with a hug and a kiss. Tell him how pleased you are that he took time away from his work to be with you.

This is not the time to bring up problems or even talk about your day. Instead, try to elicit information from him. Don't poke into those office politics you love to hear about. Instead, be prepared to listen to whatever he has to say, even if it's the workings of the internal combustion engine. Smile, nod, pass the bread. Remember, you're romancing him.

If he talks about how he's pressed for time, you can ask him about his project. If he worries about his boss breathing down his neck, you can ask him how that makes him feel. If he doesn't say anything, ask him how his food tastes. Offer him a forkful of yours. Tell him something wonderful about the way he looks right now. Compliment him on something he did recently. Tell him how you enjoy wearing the earrings he gave you (which, of course, you are wearing). Stay in the present.

Make eye contact. Flirt, wink, touch his thigh under the table, if you like. Or simply listen. If you make this enjoyable for him, he will want to do it more often. And if this new point of contact becomes a regular part of your relationship, it will create a stronger connection. A meeting place away from the stresses of home life provides freedom to express yourselves and time to keep current on each other's lives.

When it's time to leave, thank him for meeting you. Pay the check (after all, you invited him). Give him a hug. Tell him you look forward to seeing him again this evening (or whenever next time is).

In a few weeks, do it again.

One day you might even take the afternoon off.

Initiate a Little Afternoon Delight

If your partner was open to your luncheon rendezvous—especially if he was willing to take time from work to meet you—plan to have a little love-in on a weekday when you'll have your place to yourselves. (If you have children, make sure they'll be in school or day care or with a baby-sitter.)

Arrange for your partner to meet you at home. (You might want to call him at work on the morning of the appointed day and tell him that you're anxious to be with him.) If your tryst is to include food, plan an array of light snacks to take to bed with you.

Before he arrives, make sure that the room where you expect to spend your time together is clean and tidy. Then make yourself ready. If you have time, take a warm bath. Luxuriate in the feel of your body. Imagine his fingers on your skin. Play soft romantic music—or hard rock—whatever makes you feel sexy. Think of the best lovemaking you have ever had with your partner. Will it to happen again.

Be as wild as you dare. You might dress up in sexy lingerie or a fantasy outfit, or wear your business clothes and do a slow strip for him down to the sexy stuff.

If the sounds of nature can be heard through your bedroom window (birdsong, for example, or a thunderstorm), open the window. If not, you might want to put on the kind of music that makes you feel sexy. Men generally don't mind daylight for lovemaking, but do whatever is necessary to make *yourself* feel relaxed and comfortable.

Most important, focus on the moment. Limit your conversation to the two of you together right now. If your partner starts talking about his day or his concerns, put your fingers to his lips with a "shhh" or give him a kiss or ask him to unbutton your blouse. You can talk about everything else later.

Activities to Hone Your Romantic Spirit

- Greet your partner in a loving way each time you arrive home (or when he arrives, if you're there first). Let him know that you missed him during the day. Spend time focusing on the moment—on the two of you right now. Let him know that he is number one with you.

- Have a quiet, clean space in which you and your partner can relax. (See chapter 6, "Managing Time . . . Reaching Goals," for tips about keeping your space that way.) You'll make romance points just by sitting quietly beside him while he watches the news or reads the paper. Ask for nothing in return.
- Plan a special meal at home. Do it as a surprise for your partner, or plan it together. You can prepare the meal yourself, prepare it together, pick it up, or have it delivered. Send the kids to your neighbor's or to bed. Put on romantic music. Dim the lights and light the candles. Make the most of the mood. Live in the moment. If anything goes wrong, don't let it upset you; let it pass. Focus on pleasure. Smile.
- If you don't already engage in stimulating activities in the evening, find something new to pursue together at least once a week. Play a game, start a project, take a walk, learn a language, bake bread.
- Become the new woman in his life. Start flirting with him. Do it on a regular basis. Lead him on a flirty little chase, knowing that you're the prize he's after.
- Set up a luncheon meeting. Arrange it with him ahead of time. Wear something he likes to see you in, and greet him with a hug and kiss. Don't talk about work; don't say how rushed you are to get back to something (even if he does). Live in the moment. Enjoy his company. Let him see the best of you. Before you part, tell him how much you enjoyed this rendezvous. Thank him for taking time from his work to spend with you.
- Surprise your partner with some afternoon delight. Drop a few hints about what might take place so that he'll be ready. Dare to be special. He's there because he wants you. Relax and live in the moment.
- Take advantage of the weather. Bundle up and have a snowball fight in a winter storm. Share an umbrella as you splash through the April rain. Hold each other against the October winds. On a clear, warm night, hold

hands under the stars. The weather is all around you. Don't let it go unnoticed.

Creating Special Time Away

Since the daily humdrum of life is what gets in the way of romance, it's no surprise that man's romantic fantasy is to escape with the woman he loves. In fact, nearly 100 percent of the men who responded to the open-ended question "What is your romantic fantasy?" described an escape with their partner.

Whether the escape is something *you* plan or something *he* plans, certain elements are common to nearly all: remote location, sensual scene and activity, open-mindedness of both partners, lack of expectations, possibilities for eroticism, and sharing. Here are some examples from survey respondents:

"Enjoying a beautiful meal at a subdued restaurant, slow dancing to smooth jazz, and an evening that ends spending the night in each other's arms."

"Making love in a deep forest out in the open air."

"Spending a week in Venice taking moonlit gondola rides, just poking around, and making love."

"Being on an island, just the two of us."

"A vacation somewhere, being strangers together, experiencing new things together."

"A weekend alone with my lover in a mountain cabin. No skiing, no sledding, no snowboarding. Nothing to do but make love and talk, read to each other in bed, and cuddle by the fire."

"Role-playing in a medieval or Oriental setting."

"Kissing at sunset on a deserted beach."

"Coming home to find an invitation to dinner. She sets the itinerary for the evening, including the lovemaking."

"My romantic fantasy is to start over. Erase the slate. I'd like to meet my wife someplace as if she were a total stranger, take her on a few dates, and ask her to marry me all over again."

"Making love for two or three days straight."

"A nice getaway, maybe on a sailboat, to a tropical island."

"A candlelit dinner, preferably at a restaurant, to be followed by a moonlit walk on the beach and then back home, together alone, where we would massage each other with coconut oil and make love all night."

"A hike up a mountain and then making love on the mountaintop in the moonlight."

"A weekend alone in an isolated place with nothing to do but spend time together, enjoying each other's company."

You can see the similarities—freshness of scene, new beginnings. Some men offered detailed fantasies that brought together a number of common romantic desires. Here's a fun example:

"In autumn, we check into a fine historic hotel in New Orleans or maybe Charleston, in a suite with two bedrooms. The rooms are very plush with thick carpet and fine furnishings. We settle in, and she wants to take a leisurely bath, so I go to the hotel lounge and get a drink. When I return, she comes to my room dressed in a very sexy, somewhat revealing outfit. She speaks to me as if we don't know each other. We go out to dinner—candles, wine, flowers, music. We go to a play—a romantic comedy. Following the play, we take a leisurely ride in a carriage through the historic section of town, snuggling together against the night chill. After a great evening, she invites me back to her (our) hotel room for some wine. She puts on some soft jazz, opens the curtains overlooking the city, and comes on to me really strong. She seduces me, taking complete charge of the situation. She tells me what to do and how she wants it done."

A tropical island would be great for a special occasion, but spending wads of money isn't necessary. You could fulfill your partner's romantic fantasy with a getaway weekend to a local spot—a campsite in the mountains, a cabin by the lake, or a hotel in the city. The point is to get rid of the distractions that interfere with romance and take time out to focus on each other.

You might want to draw out your own partner's romantic fantasies and begin to plan for a big getaway. But in the meantime, you can do a lot of romancing his way without ever leaving town.

As you attempt to romance your partner and increase the romance in your relationship, however, keep in mind that some of the greatest disappointments result from unfulfilled expectations. In order to avoid this pitfall, a good motto is "Expect nothing and be prepared for whatever might happen." A special rendezvous, for example, can be a disappointment if you expect only the magical. Maybe magic will happen (and won't that be grand), but where human emotions are involved, you cannot prescribe an outcome. Instead, use your sense of humor and your imagination to get through the rough spots so that you and your partner can enjoy special times together no matter what occurs. Perfect situations are rare, but fortunately for all of us, romance doesn't require perfection. So just plan to have fun.

Treat Him to a Romantic Dinner

A romantic dinner requires an intimate mood, which can be created in a restaurant, in a meadow, or on a mountaintop. The two prerequisites for such intimacy are being away from all distractions and focusing on each other for an extended and unrushed period of time.

For starters, choose a romantic atmosphere. A restaurant divided into small, cozy rooms can set a romantic mood, but a converted old barn may offer its own kind of charm. The choice depends on what you and your partner most enjoy.

A restaurant set by the ocean or on a mountainside can be special, but what's inside the door matters most. Consider the lighting, the music, the noise level. Are the tables spaced far enough apart to allow for intimate conversation? Are there linen napkins on the tables? (Does it matter?) Maybe there's a cocktail lounge with a dance band. Maybe there's a window with a view. Check everything out ahead of time. Make reservations far in advance so you can choose your seating time. If there's a special section or table where you would like to be seated, make sure that's part of your reservation.

Service is important. You'll want a restaurant where your server is alert to your needs—always there when needed, but never intruding. A romantic restaurant will appreciate that you and your partner want to spend time lingering over your meal. Make sure you choose a place where you won't be told that others are waiting for your table.

Soft, slow music helps set the mood, as long as it's music both you and your partner like. Live music can add a special touch, and a dance floor is a romantic plus if you both like to dance.

Don't overlook the quality of the food, for this is key to a successful evening. Check out restaurant reviews in your local newspaper, ask friends whose taste you can trust, or go to the restaurant by yourself to sample the food. Be sure that it's a type and style of cuisine that your partner will also enjoy. If you're unsure, ask him. Take the time and the initiative to find a special place that he will like.

Conversation can make or break a romantic dinner. Focus on the present and on your relationship. Avoid any topics that will cause distress. If your partner starts talking about work or chores or difficulties, gently bring the conversation back to the moment—to the food, to how good he looks, to how great it is to be here with him. While he speaks, make eye contact. Show interest when he shares new thoughts or ideas with you.

And if you invited him out for this romantic evening, when the bill comes, it's yours (you might want to discreetly let your server know ahead of time).

In order to prolong the romance, don't schedule anything to do after dinner. A romantic dinner is romantic in itself. Rushing off to a play, a movie, or a game could take the romance out of your dinner date.

But that doesn't mean you must go straight home. Appropriate activities to follow a romantic dinner are those that do not require a timed arrival—walk to a rooftop bar for a nightcap, drop in on a romantic dancing spot, drive to the shore or a high point overlooking the city. Whatever you do, don't rush. Romance is living in the present.

If you can't swing the expense of a night out, or if you have a new baby, create a romantic dinner at home. In fact, you can create a romantic dinner anywhere. Even a picnic in the backyard can be romantic if the food is enjoyable and you focus on each other.

Get Away

There is nothing like a change of scenery to help a couple break out of their routine and find romance. Just getting away from the household cares can be a freeing experience for you both. A majority of survey respondents wrote about the delights of going away with their partner. Some liked to plan the escape themselves, but most were ready for a spontaneous weekend getaway whenever the invitation appeared.

One man described his romantic fantasy this way: "On a Friday after getting out of work, get in a jeep and spend a weekend in the woods, sleeping with the moon as a ceiling and enjoying each other."

Take their advice and take the initiative. To fulfill your partner's romantic fantasy, whisk him away from the distractions of home life to a place where you can focus totally on one another. You could plan something for a special occasion, such as his birthday. But why wait? Romance happens anytime. If you get out and play together, you'll come home with a much more romantic outlook on your relationship.

Like the romantic dinner, romantic getaways can take many forms—some costly, some not. If you live in the country, a few days in the city might be exciting. If you live in a city, you may want to head for the hills. It's important to plan something your partner will enjoy, but be sure that *you* want to do it, too.

Nearly 60 percent of men surveyed rated "Participate in my hobbies or interests" as important to their love relationship; the rating was highest (65 percent) for men with children living at home. What interests do you and your partner share? Where can you go to enjoy them together?

If you live in a college or university town, you have rich opportunities to enjoy music, sports, theater, and lectures. These events usually aren't well publicized, so call the school to find out what's happening. Many communities offer civic events, such as plays, concerts, and games at very reasonable prices. So when you can't swing the cost of symphony tickets or a trip to Broadway, try a concert in the park, a local performance at your university or community college, or even a classic movie at the cinema.

For an overnight trip, would your partner rather stay at a hotel in a big city or in a sleeping bag under the stars? Many books available in local libraries and bookstores provide details on the locations, amenities, and prices of getaways for a variety of interests and budgets. Auto clubs, such as the American Automobile Association, offer their members information about inexpensive driving vacations. Friends and coworkers may also have suggestions. Major newspapers (in the Sunday travel section, for example) publish articles as well as advertisements on fun places to visit. In addition, you can check with a travel agency, where you will find free maps, brochures, and advice. By the way, your partner may have his own ideas about places to go. So be sure to ask him.

When checking out specific locations, find out the particulars. Even the most romantic places have at least a few rooms that aren't romantic at all. Check out the noise level, the size of the bed, and any possible distractions. Depending on the situation, you may want to reserve a particular room or a room on a certain side of the building (the one with the view, perhaps?).

And what about amenities? Is breakfast included? How about a good restaurant on the premises or nearby? Can someone pack you a picnic for an afternoon hike? Can you rent a boat to row around the lake? Is there a pool? A tennis court? A golf course? Or maybe an intimate hot tub for two? Is there a park or woodsy area where you can take a secluded walk or bike ride? What about a quiet little bar with soft music for slow dancing?

When you make the reservations, be sure to ask about local highlights, activities, and restaurants as well. And when you arrive at your destination, ask your host for recommendations on things to do.

You don't have to do all the planning yourself—your partner may prefer to make some of the decisions—but he'll appreciate it if you take the lead and follow through on the details.

Involve Children

If you have children living at home, it is critical that you spend time together as a family. As a matter of fact, men with children living at home rated "Arrange for us to be together as a family" of higher importance (88 percent) than "Spend time with me away from the children" (82 percent). Both are vital to the health of your relationship.

Although you may prefer to separate the two, there are many options for integrating romance into family vacations. One such option is to plan your vacation at a place that offers care and activities for children. This allows you to spend time together as a family and also to take time out for relaxing alone with your partner, knowing that your children are having fun on their own. The YMCA and the Sierra Club are two of many organizations that offer such vacations (if your local branch doesn't offer these options, check with the national headquarters). Club Med provides baby care at some of its resorts and supervised teen activities at others. Major hotels, cruise lines, and sporting clubs are increasingly offering such services. Your local library should be of help in finding sources, and a good travel agent will be able to advise you.

An organization called TWYCH (Travel with Your Children) publishes a newsletter with information about where to vacation with your children, including reviews of sites and activities. You can reach TWYCH at 80 Eighth Avenue, New York, New York 10011, phone 212/206-0688.

With a little up-front planning, you'll find that many roads lead to romance.

Activities to Hone Your Romantic Spirit

• For a special dinner out, learn about romantic dining spots in your area. Spend a little time: go to each one, look at the menu, ask about dinnertime lighting and music, take a peek at the plates coming from the kitchen, notice the dining room arrangement, and determine which table you would like to reserve.

• Take note when your partner says, "Gee, I'd like to...." In addition, you might want to mention some things you believe he would enjoy, or some things you would enjoy, just to prompt a reaction. When the time comes to make a plan, be sure to ask him if this is what he wants. If he seems hesitant, have him suggest something else, or present him with a list of options you think he would enjoy and let him choose.

• Start planning. Check the newspapers, the yellow pages, and travel agencies. Ask your friends for recommendations. Check books and magazines that focus on your partner's favorite activities. (The back pages of his own magazines may have ads for holidays focused on his preferred activities or interests.)

• Determine how much you can spend. Is this getaway going to be for one night, a weekend, a week, or longer?

• Check your schedules, and begin to actualize your plan.

• If you have children to consider, look into the various alternatives that will allow you to travel as a family yet spend romantic time alone with your partner.

Giving Him Time Off

The greatest conflicts in love relationships revolve around two opposing needs: the need to be close and the need to be free. Resolution depends in part on how you spend your time.

If your partner wants to spend time away from you, it doesn't mean that he isn't committed to you. Survey responses bear this out. One example:

> "It's important to me that we each have a separate space. Sometimes that means that I go to the backyard to garden while she works in the office, and sometimes it means that one of us works in the kitchen while the other takes a walk. We have separate friends and interests as well as mutual friends and interests. After going off on our separate courses, we each have more to offer when we come together again. I love being in the same space with my wife, but one of the reasons that our marriage has worked so well for us so long may just be that we are not afraid to spend time apart."

An important finding from the survey was the male imperative to spend time away from the relationship—either alone or "with the guys." More than 60 percent of men surveyed rated "Give me free time away without complaint" as important to their love relationship. They also said that it didn't happen often enough.

If you feel unloved or abandoned each time your partner takes off with his friends, it is important that you find ways to fulfill yourself when alone. If you are accomplishing household chores while your partner is playing, you will probably resent your partner's time off. You may not want to spend time with your friends while your partner is with his, but there are certainly many things other than chores that you would like to do, and this may be the time to do them. (Chapter 6, "Managing Time . . . Reaching Goals," discusses ways to bring balance to your life so that you can pursue your own goals and activities.)

Allow Him the Time He Needs

Your partner may spend his time away from you with other people, or he may be happiest going off alone to jog or ride his bicycle. If he doesn't invite you along, don't pout. He needs this time to himself. In riding his bicycle, for example, he might be measuring his speed or distance with each ride, competing with his own previous record. Or maybe he's just clearing his mind. If you want to go along on a bike ride, that's something you can plan for another time.

This isn't to imply that a man must spend his solitary time away from home. He may have favorite activities, such as woodworking, playing computer games, or fixing the car. What you don't want to do is follow him around, asking him to help you with something or trying to make conversation. If you do that, he is likely to take his laptop or that car he is fixing down to the local park, where you can't bother him. Basically, he needs time to get away from daily concerns; conversation with you might not be the best way for him to do that. In fact, men surveyed said that they are more inclined to give time to their partners, their relationships, and their households if they are allowed a time-out on a regular basis.

Even if your partner is committed to helping with household chores and maintenance, if you hold him captive, slave to your "honey, do" list, he will be resentful. When there are special chores that you would like him to do, you can let him know (a list is fine). Include the date or time that the chores need to be completed, if that's important. Then let your partner do them his own way on his own time. If you're always looking over his shoulder, ready to criticize or micromanage him, or if you've always got just one more thing for him to do, he will resent doing anything.

If you want him to come back, you've got to let him go.

Coordinate Schedules

It's important that you coordinate the use of your time apart. Let your partner schedule his tennis match on his own time and do the chores when it's most convenient for him. If you are going to entertain your own friends at home, or if you would like quiet time at home by yourself, you'll want to make sure that your plans don't conflict with those of your partner.

If you have children, you need to schedule time to spend together as a family. But in order to take time on your own as well, you must coordinate schedules. Here you have a few alternatives for arranging your own time off. The first is to get someone to watch the children for a few hours while you and your partner each go off to pursue independent activities. If you don't want to hire a baby-sitter, you may be able to swap baby-sitting with a neighbor—you take care of the neighbor's children once a week, and they take yours once a week. If you want to spend time working out at a gym, look for one with a good child-care facility. If you want to take yourself to lunch with your favorite book or poke around the shops, look for a shopping mall that offers quality child care.

A better alternative might be for you and your partner to alternate your time off so that each of you has special time alone with the children. In this way, you will each get to know the children on your own terms, and the children will benefit from the special relationships that will develop.

Make the Most of Your Own Time

Whether you work away from home, in your own home-based business, or your work is at home with your children, there are always scads of things that must be done. Cooking, cleaning, laundry, shopping: the list is endless. And even if a man contributes time and energy to keeping up the household, it's generally the woman who holds ultimate responsibility. Thus you may feel guilty going off to play while there are still things left to do.

Yet the truth is, there will always be more to do. And the suffering servant is definitely not romantic. If your "to do" list keeps you from taking time for yourself, your resentment will show through loud and clear. Everyone needs time away from the family—to think, to relax, to rejuvenate. And that includes you.

According to survey results, your partner agrees that you need this time. More than 80 percent of men surveyed said it's important to the relationship that their partner pursue her own interests.

Depending on your own desires, this may mean meeting with friends, exercising, taking classes, or just relaxing alone in a quiet place. You'll have much more to give your partner if you allow yourself regular time-outs.

Activities to Hone Your Romantic Spirit

- Ask your partner whether he feels he spends enough time "with the guys" or "doing his own thing." If he says no, find out what's going on. Does he feel guilty about leaving you with the chores? Does he lack motivation or energy? Whatever the reason, help him to schedule more time for himself. You'll have a better relationship for it.
- If your partner doesn't have any interests other than his work, help him to get involved in something new. Find out what sorts of things he has dreamed about doing, and encourage him to start in on them. A new hobby or sport may mean taking a course or signing up with a club or team; a new interest might be developed through volunteer work. Once he's involved, be as supportive as you can.
- If your partner doesn't take time for physical exercise, invite him on a walk every evening or persuade him to go for a bike ride with you on weekends. Encourage him to get into an exercise program at your local community center or gym. This is part of the nurturing he needs from you. Help him take care of himself.
- Acknowledge your partner's role in household chores and maintenance, and thank him for what he does. Tell him you feel his love when he does these things for you. But let him do them on his own terms.
- If you and your partner schedule activities away from each other, touch base at least once a week to coordinate your plans and learn about any changes.
- If you have children living at home, coordinate plans for their care—either take turns with them, hire some help, or find some time when the children will be away (at school, camp, Scouts, whatever).

- If you keep a "to do" list for yourself, start entering time-outs on it. Schedule at least two hours each week. If any-one asks how you can go off and leave your messy house to read a trashy novel in the park, just tell them it's your mental health break. You'll have more to give, and you'll be a better friend, mother, lover, and nurturer for it.
- If you don't get enough peer time, make plans to meet your friends, coworkers, or neighbors occasionally to share feelings and information. Meet them for lunch, for coffee after work, or for a walk on the weekend—what-ever is most convenient.
- Start thinking about new interests you might pursue in your newfound time off. And look forward to reading chapter 6, "Managing Time . . . Reaching Goals," which will help you create an action plan to carry them out.
- Be sure to thank your partner for his part in helping you find the time.

4

Fueling the Flame

Sex provides the ultimate union for partners both to give and to receive love and joy. Sex can be serious, passionate, playful, tender, or all these things at once. Unfortunately, there has been so much public discussion of sexual expectations that couples may be wondering if they are missing something.

If we look to the characters portrayed in romance novels and movies as sexual role models, we will expect men to think of sex at all times, to have erections at a moment's notice, to be in total control of any sexual situation, and to perform anywhere, anytime, and under any condition. And, of course, we will expect them to have their partners screaming in ecstasy every time. For lack of other role models, these characters have become the elusive goal, even though we know that they aren't real. To believe that such fantasy is possible, however, can do great harm to an otherwise wonderful relationship, causing men to feel less than adequate and causing women to question whether they are getting what they deserve.

According to survey respondents, a lot of great sex is happening out there. But you cannot expect every sexual encounter to be exciting. In fact, sex can be downright boring.

There are, however, many ways in which you can enhance your sexual relationship. It may take a little extra attention to your own needs as well as to the needs of your partner. But life's too short to miss out here. Add a little romance, and you're on your way to a more loving, fulfilling sex life.

To that end, this chapter offers numerous ideas, activities, and exercises. But do not feel compelled to try them all. Some may be embarrassing for you; others may seem too erotic or even demeaning. You and your partner have a unique relationship, and only the two of you can determine appropriate sexual activity. Nevertheless, if you approach this chapter with an open mind, you may find yourself becoming receptive to new ways of both giving and enjoying sexual pleasure.

Bringing Out His Sexy Best

The romantic fantasies men described in their survey responses often included sex. And more than 65 percent of men surveyed said it's important that their partner "attend to my sexual needs." Unfortunately, many men stated that they were not satisfied in this area.

Even if you and your partner already enjoy a satisfying sexual relationship, you can still enhance your pleasure by finding out what pleases each of you most.

Learn What Pleases

In a loving, trusting relationship, sex is an opportunity to open up and allow yourself to discover the extent of your partner's desires as well as your own. But one of the problems of believing in the fantasy role model is that men may not express what they need to enhance their own sexual experiences.

In *The New Male Sexuality,* Dr. Bernie Zilbergeld writes:

> Many men have little idea of what they like in sex and dismiss the question with a blanket "it all feels good." If you think it all feels the same, you can do a lot to improve your sex life by challenging that notion. It's inconceivable that a hard touch feels exactly as pleasurable as a soft touch, or that long kisses feel exactly the same as pecks on the cheek. The problem, I think, is that we men are so busy performing that many of us haven't taken the time to determine what pleasures us the most. If you want to find out more about what feels best to you, get your partner to do different things.

. . . Focus in on the sensations and see how you feel. That's all there is to it. Doing this over a period of weeks will give you more information about what you like.

Encourage your partner to discover what pleases him. One of the most fun-filled ways is the "trial-and-pleasure" technique: Try it and see if he likes it. Here are some of the things you'll want to explore.

- What helps him relax? Possibilities might include quiet space, time to unwind, comfortable clothing, music, a favorite food or drink, massage.
- What helps him feel more connected to you? Sitting close, holding hands, touching, eye contact, feeding each other.
- What stimulates his senses? Your clean body scent, soft skin and hair, a cozy atmosphere, romantic lighting, certain music, food and drink, touching, touchable fabrics, perfume.
- What arouses his desire? Sexy clothing, kissing, touching, erotic pictures and stories, body rubbing, whispering sexy words, undressing each other, dancing, varied rooms or environments, danger of being "caught."
- What helps him feel confident? Praise, attention, compliments.
- What helps him feel safe to ask for what he wants? Acceptance, positive response, attention, your listening without judgment or demands.
- What satisfies him best? Different types of touching, kissing, various positions, a range of physical stimulation.

Some couples have found value in literally interviewing each other as if they were sociologists rather than lovers. It's an artificial situation, to be sure, but if you ask your partner questions without assuming anything about him—as though he were a stranger—and without interpreting his responses as referring to you, you could garner useful information to help you significantly increase his sexual pleasure.

Although you should be ready to experiment, be sure to stay within your own comfort zone, and take it slowly. And to keep him comfortable, don't judge. You're asking your partner to open up and be vulnerable; your reactions to his desires will either encourage him to open up further or cause him to shun future communication on the subject.

With some prompting and encouragement, you should be able to find a combination of activities that works well—activities that the two of you can mix and match for pleasurable variety. And you may just discover that your partner desires a lot of the same things that you do.

Express Yourself

To get the greatest enjoyment from sex, you need to know and express what *you* want. Know what conditions are important for you to feel sexy—time of day, place, lighting, clothing, food, foreplay, atmosphere. Also, learn what makes you feel satisfied. If you let your partner know these things, and if he follows through, your increased enjoyment will increase his pleasure as well. For as Dr. John Gray says, in *Mars and Venus in the Bedroom,* "If a woman has a great time, the man tends to take credit, and it excites him even more. His fulfillment and pleasure are ensured by her fulfillment."

A couple's love grows, changes, and matures over time, and their sexual relationship grows and changes as well. Each sexual encounter will probably be different. Sometimes sex is serious and passionate, sometimes it's playful, and sometimes it incorporates a range of feelings and expressions. But there is no right way. In fact, one of the beauties of a long-term love relationship is the continuous discovery of new ways of enjoying sex over time.

If affection, honesty, and trust infuse your relationship, you should be able to explore your own sexuality as well as your partner's. If you are reticent about discussing what you need, however, try something like, "I get really turned on when you pay special attention to me. I love it when you [fill in the blank].” Be specific. If you want him to set a mood, remind him of the time he seduced you with the lights low and music playing and whatever else he did that pleased you. If you want him to dance with you, sing to you, or spend special time cuddling on the couch with you, remind him of the times when he did those things. Reinforce the positive, and you'll get more of it.

Just a word or two, or a sound of pleasure, should give your partner enough information during sex to help him please you. As one man wrote: “To be able to offer my partner complete sexual satisfaction, witnessing her bodily joy in erotic stimulation—that makes me feel special.”

Praise His Style

Every man needs to know that the woman he loves wants him sexually. And he needs to know that he can delight her with sexual pleasure.

Because you are your partner's lover, friend, and ally, he wants you to let him know that he is strong and good and capable of bringing you rapture. This point was underlined by men responding to the survey question “Has there ever been a time when a partner made you feel really special?” Some examples:

“Yes, when my partner told me I was a good lover.”

“Occasionally, after we make love, she tells me that she feels very lucky, that I am really something else. This makes me feel great. . . . feed my male ego!”

“When she let me know that I satisfy her sexual needs.”

“Yes, when my partner let me know that I had given her intense pleasure.”

Whenever your partner does give you pleasure, let him know right away. Don't hide your physical or emotional response.

If you want him to do something differently or try something new, show or tell him in a positive way. Receive his romantic gestures gratefully, and he'll keep trying. Show him that you are open to *his* suggestions, as well.

According to Dr. Gerald Smith, a common idea in our culture is that it's the man's job to bring the woman to orgasm. It's as though the woman is some kind of musical instrument and the man is supposed to tune the instrument to a perfect pitch. This puts a great deal of pressure on the man to perform, and because of the demands it puts on the woman, it sets up the common practice of faking orgasms. A person's sexual pleasure is the property of the person who's having the experience and is not anyone else's responsibility. In a good relationship, the two people want to respond to each other as best they can, but the man does not have ownership of the woman's response. The purpose of sex is intimacy, not orgasm.

Fun and passion will come spontaneously from a close relationship in which the partners are interdependent rather than independent. If your partner knows that you think of him as special, he will probably feel special when he's with you, which in turn will increase his pleasure with your company both in and out of bed. It's up to you to let him know that he is not only desired but also desirable.

Look Your Best

Nearly 80 percent of men surveyed said it is important to them that their partner "keep herself looking clean and attractive." Greeting him at the door with nothing but a ribbon around your waist and a smile is not the answer. If that's fun for you, fine. But more important is for you to look your best for him on a continuing basis. Is this sexist? No, it's a matter of priority.

You probably spend time grooming before going to your job, before seeing your friends, or before a night on the town. Your partner certainly deserves as much. This isn't just to excite him when you want sex but to maintain your partner's visual interest over the long term.

While women are aroused by sensations related predominantly to touch and hearing, men are more often aroused by visual stimuli. Men can be "turned on" by even the sight of female bodies in suggestive postures or clothing.

Of course, every man is an individual, and you need to discover what pleases your own partner. If he really does love to see you in your baggy old sweats, okay. But chances are he would probably rather see you in a soft blouse or sweater, and feminine slacks, shorts, or a skirt. If you don't know what your partner prefers, experiment with different outfits or styles, and gauge his reaction. Pay attention to what he notices about your various looks.

Most women think they need to lose weight (whether or not they actually do), but most men don't care that their partner doesn't have what she considers a perfect body. Certainly you want to look as good as you can, but don't let a little flab or a few wrinkles or gray hairs keep you from being the best that you are right now. In the men's survey, flab did not appear as an issue. Gray's findings bear this out: "When a man loves you, the more aroused he becomes, the more perfect your body becomes to him. The last thing on a man's mind during sex is how fat your thighs are."

Although about 80 percent of men surveyed said that it's important for their partner to "keep herself in good physical condition," it seems that men and women have differing opinions about the word *good*. More than a few men bemoaned the fact that their partner feels inhibited because her body isn't perfect. One example: "I would like my partner to be a little more confident about herself, and take my compliments more seriously. She's a great-looking woman, and I'm lucky to have her, but she's not entirely happy with her appearance. When she dresses up even just a little, she's a knockout, and I'd like her to know and feel how proud I am to be with her. I'm trying to figure out how, but telling her doesn't seem to be the answer. She's extremely intelligent and driven, and has set very high standards for herself. So high that she apparently doesn't even know when she's hit some of them."

Envious of her? Don't be. That just may be what your own partner thinks about you.

When women are able to get beyond their own sense of their bodies, they can find new ways to please their partners. Another survey response illustrates this: "My partner has always been very self-conscious of her body, especially her tush. She routinely shies away from revealing negligees. But she surprised me one night by wearing a thong. For me, it was special because I knew she did it to please me. And of course it did! So now she's not afraid to wear all sorts of sexy things for me, which I appreciate."

By all means, keep yourself in good physical shape. If you feel good about your body, you'll feel sexy. If you feel sexy, you'll act sexy. If you act sexy, you'll be more likely to please your partner as well as yourself. You'll want to show off your body to him. You'll let go of inhibitions related to your looks. You'll elicit passion and romance.

But try not to get hung up on wanting to look like a cover girl. After all, when you take away the makeup, the hairstyling, and the photographer's airbrush, these perfect creatures don't actually exist. If you keep yourself looking as good as you can while accepting yourself as you are, your partner is sure to appreciate your self-confidence.

Activities to Hone Your Romantic Spirit

- Help your partner discover what pleases him. Encourage him to explore ways of relaxing. Learn how you can help him feel confident, connected, and safe enough to ask for what he wants. Use the trial-and-pleasure method to discover what stimulates his senses, arouses his desires, satisfies him.

- Do you know what pleases you? If you don't, ask your partner to try some of the same techniques you used to find out what pleases him. Give him feedback when he pleases you. If you have ideas about what you would like him to try, let him know.

- Obtain a copy of Dr. Miriam Stoppard's *The Magic of Sex,* and page through it with your partner while you both comment on things that might be fun to try.
- Are you open to new experiences? While staying within your own comfort level, start fantasizing about what might make your sexual relationship more exciting. Once you feel comfortable enough to try something new, suggest it to your partner—or initiate it yourself.
- If you and your partner have different desires in sex, try negotiating. If you do "this" for him, he'll be more likely to do "that" for you. By developing such a give-and-take, you will not only please each other, but you will also find common ground.
- If your partner wants sex more often than you do, try a little mental stimulation before your next get-together, and hold that thought. Set a mood that will help you relax and feel sexy. Encourage him to take part in whatever it is that arouses you.
- Tell your partner everything great about his lovemaking style—everything you appreciate about how he makes you feel. And you'll be assured of getting more.

Getting Involved

From the survey, the message came through loud and clear: Men want their partners to take a more active role in lovemaking. More than 50 percent of men surveyed (75 percent of those with children) said it's important for their partner to "show off her body for me." More than 70 percent (85 percent of those with children) wanted their partner to "act sexy when we're alone together." And nearly 80 percent of all survey respondents said it's important that their partner "initiate sex."

What is particularly telling, however, is that the majority of these men claim that they aren't being satisfied in this key area.

So, if your relationship is at all typical of theirs, here's a real opportunity to add sparkle.

Initiate Sex

"Women seem to think that men have it all," wrote one survey respondent. "But in the relationship game, men have the raw deal. Men have to do all the initiating, all the pleasing, all the romancing. And a woman can take it or leave it. Women don't understand that men want to be respected and appreciated for their romantic efforts—no matter how meager those efforts may seem. Some things take a lot of guts. It would be nice to see a little of what you call 'romance' coming in our direction."

By initiating sex, a woman lets her partner know that she wants *him*. She also demonstrates that she is ready and willing, which then saves him from another rejection. Sure, she takes a little risk, but in doing so, she becomes very sexy.

After all, why should the man always be the one to decide when to do it? A healthier relationship exists when both partners feel free to either suggest or decline sex at any given time. In essence, a *yes* cannot be a true *yes* unless *no* is also available.

A number of survey respondents wrote of their pleasure when their partner initiated sex:

"My partner makes me feel special when she tries to please me first."

"It always pleases me when she puts on something slightly revealing and sort of flirts around the edges. She doesn't have to come out and say, 'I want you,' because I can feel it."

"The most erotic thing a woman can do is let you know—in her own style—that she wants you."

"My romantic fantasy is to be looked after sexually for just one night."

"What are the times when she makes me feel special? Whenever she seduces me!"

Depending on your partner's experiences and expectations in your relationship, initiating sex may be as simple as giving

him a special look, a lingering good-night kiss, or a strategi-
cally placed touch. And if you have spent some time discover-
ing what your partner desires, use the things you learned to
excite him. But if you want to be more dramatic and make your
partner know you mean business, there are lots of ways.

One way to increase your own sexual desire is to hold on to
sexual fantasies that occur to you during the day. For example,
if you hear a song on the radio that gives rise to sexual arousal
or longing, ride with it. Fantasize about it. Then, every few
hours throughout the day, revisit those feelings. Don't let them
go. By the time you see your partner, you'll be wanting the sex
that he's been wanting.

In addition, if you have the time, set a mood for yourself
with lighting, music, sexy clothing—anything that makes you
feel more relaxed, more confident, more open to new experiences. Take a bath in scented salts and luxuriate in the feel of
your own skin. Focus on your fantasy. Change it in any way
that pleases you. Do whatever makes you feel sexier, and you
and your partner will both reap the benefits.

Take care of your appearance. According to survey respondents, a woman shouldn't worry about looking like a runway
model, but she should be clean and touchable with sweet-
smelling breath and hair. Attending to your appearance will
help you feel more confident in your come-on. And confidence
itself can be an aphrodisiac.

Wear something that makes you feel sexy—clothes that are
somewhat revealing, soft to the touch, and easy to slip off.

Creating a space for just the two of you and setting up a romantic atmosphere is a cue you could try—a candle or oil lamp
in the bedroom, romantic music, perfume. More than half the
survey respondents rated the statement "Create a sexy atmosphere when we're alone" as important. Shut out the real world.
Let the answering machine take the calls. And most important,
never talk about anything that has anything to do with anything
other than making love. If you attempt to bring up daily concerns, disappointments, expectations, or something else that's irrelevant to this seduction scene, you can forget about romance.

Attitude is important. Make it fun. Think of a sexy smile, a come-hither look. Imagine yourself as the sexiest woman alive, and your face will show it.

Flirting adds to the fun. Make advances with eye contact, smiles, winks, little touches. Sweet-talk him by speaking in low, sensual tones or whispering sexy compliments into his ear. The nonverbal behavior that comes naturally with flirting may be even more effective in sending messages than the words themselves. Lean toward him, play with your hair, touch your clothes or body.

Dramatically taking off a piece of your clothing will not go unnoticed. You could follow this by unbuttoning his shirt and massaging his chest. Nibble on his ear. Kiss his neck. Run your fingers through his hair. Give him lingering touches. Maybe even bring his hand to your breast.

You might dance for him, removing a garment or two as you do, exposing a bit of bare flesh. (Let him finish undressing you.) Or try undressing him, stroking and kissing him all over as you go.

If you feel uncomfortable or foolish with such subtle techniques, just come right out and tell him what you want. As Tom Hanks said so enthusiastically in the movie *Big:* "I get to be on top!"

But whatever your come-on, reacting positively to his responses is part of your advance and will keep him coming for more. If you and your partner practice romance on a regular basis, sex will come naturally, as an organic part of the relationship.

One caveat: Expectations can quickly erode sexual and romantic energy. It's best not to attach yourself to a certain outcome. Stay in the present, and enjoy whatever it brings.

As you become more involved in initiating sex, you should learn to determine when your partner doesn't want it. Maybe he's too tired, he's too full from dinner, he doesn't feel well, or he's concerned about something outside the relationship. If you perceive that this isn't a good time for him, back off before either of you becomes hurt or disappointed.

In order to gauge how he may respond (and excite him as well), call him early in the day and give him a sexy message. Or if you're home together, go out to where he's shooting baskets or working at the computer and give him a wink and a romantic kiss. Start flirting early on. Assess his response. And get ready for a good time.

Get Passionate

Even if the man initiates sex, he wants his partner to participate. And survey respondents said they would like more participation from their partner than they are now getting. But what exactly do men want?

Show enthusiasm. During each sexual encounter, take the initiative again and again to hug, caress, and stroke your partner. Play an active role. Don't worry about how you look when you're enjoying what he is doing. Let yourself go. Make noise. Tell him how wonderful whatever he's doing makes you feel. Express your pleasures.

Get yourself into the mood. Close your eyes and think of something that turns you on. Be there. Go with it even if it's naughty. It's only in your head, so don't worry about what your partner will think. Imagine that you just picked him up at the local dance hall. Or imagine you're in a room full of people or in the backseat of a limousine or in the back room at a party or in a cow pasture—whatever turns you on. Imagine that you're having a secret, steamy affair with him. Make it as exciting and erotic as you can. Keep your eyes closed for a bit and feel it happen.

After a couple has been together for a while, the one thing they may think they can't give each other is novelty. But if you allow your imagination to run free, you can improvise and innovate, thus sparking new excitement.

A man may be shy about going all out to sexually romance a woman if he has been living with her for years. After all, he might look like a fool if his partner isn't responsive. So encourage every little gesture that points in the right direction. If he makes *any* attempt to add romance to sex, reward him with your passion. Each time he'll become more confident to go a little further with romance.

Passion includes receiving your partner's overtures openly and lovingly. As one man wrote, "It's great when she's just her sweet lovely self, willing to be romanced, enjoying being held and cuddled." That can go a long way toward a more romantic relationship.

Seize the Moment

Women who responded to the survey for *How to Romance the Woman You Love—The Way She Wants You To!* stated that they would like more spontaneous sex. But men have learned that women need plenty of foreplay and don't like quickies, and therefore men may feel unsure about initiating anything when there's only a short time available.

So this is up to you. On those occasions when you feel sexy and the two of you have at least fifteen minutes alone together, just do it.

Come on to him soft and breezy. That's the sort of thing men said they would love—soft kisses, bodies rubbing, hands all over him. Forget who you are for a moment, and just feel the electricity pulse between you.

Don't scold him if he doesn't want to or isn't ready for you. Even if sex doesn't happen right now, you just may start something simmering that will last until you're both charged up. So hold that thought!

Activities to Hone Your Romantic Spirit

- If you're not accustomed to initiating sex, start with something subtle, such as an intimate whisper or your hand on his thigh. When you get into bed, prolong your good-night kiss. If you feel daring, pull his hand to your breast or between your legs. Be aware that he may not pick up on a first, understated attempt. But that's all right. It's a start.

- Whenever you plan to approach your partner for love-making, make sure that you are clean and sweet smelling. Add to the fun by wearing something provocative— maybe something he'll discover during foreplay.
- If you're feeling sexy and you want to make sure your partner is ready when you are, drop him a hint ahead of time. Make a sexy phone call (leave a message on his private voice mail), put a suggestive little note where he's sure to find it, or whisper something seductive when you meet and then go off humming a sweet little tune until he comes to find you.
- You'll enjoy your lovemaking more if you feel confident that you look your best. Take care of yourself. But remember that your partner is not seeking the perfect body. He wants *you*.
- If you're not accustomed to flirting, practice your smiles in the mirror when you're alone. Add some growls, purrs, and whispers, and maybe even a shocking word or two. Get into it. Make it fun.
- As part of your come-on, try unbuttoning his shirt and kissing his chest. Go from there. . . .
- Create a romantic space for just the two of you with soft lighting, sexy music, perfume, little nibbles, his favorite drink. Concentrate on sensual topics. If he talks about something other than romance, gently guide the conversation back to the two of you together in this moment.
- If you don't already take an active role in your lovemaking, start today. Let your partner know what pleases you. Try different lovemaking positions and styles with him. Put his hands where you want them. Try kissing a part of his body you've never kissed before. Take some initiative. Show enthusiasm (screaming in ecstasy will get his attention). And watch him respond.
- If you have children, you'll need to be strategic about your opportunities. With small children, you can plan

your moments for when they're asleep. But as they grow, teach them the importance of privacy by letting them know that when you and your partner are in the bedroom together with the door shut, they are to leave you alone.

Recapturing the Good Times

Over time the problems, worries, and disappointments that naturally arise from day-to-day living can interfere with lovemaking. It's important to discuss such concerns with your partner, clearing the air so that you both can be open to accepting one another's love. But even during those times when the two of you haven't totally resolved a problem, meet your partner in bed with an open mind and an open heart, and you'll find your sexual relationship begin to blossom again.

Vary Lovemaking Styles

One way to keep a sexual relationship exciting over the years is to vary the styles and positions of lovemaking. Slow. Quick. Drawn out. This room. That room. On top. In front. Behind. Below.

Positions aren't as important as affection, touching, communication, caring, sensuality, and love. But your sex life can be enhanced with a little adventure and experimentation.

What do you like best in terms of timing, position, place, mood? What does your partner like? Don't limit yourself to a routine. Today do it this way, tomorrow that way, and next week try something else.

Responding to the survey for the companion book, a woman wrote: "After years of marriage, we've learned to keep sex exciting by using different kinds of ways to make love. We have our typical twenty-minute sessions, our quickies, and our special times when we create a sensual atmosphere and engage in prolonged foreplay. We have also developed 'sex vacations'—taking off together for a romantic night or weekend where we can focus on intimacy and refresh our sex life."

Don't expect your partner to make all the decisions. That leads to resentment—on his part as well as yours. If he goes for the same position and timing with each sexual encounter, try taking the lead and showing him a thing or two. Variety, as the cliché goes, is the spice of life.

There may be some sexual styles that you enjoy most and others that your partner prefers. You may need to negotiate here. But don't wait to enjoy sex until everything is perfect for both of you, or you'll be waiting a long time.

One way to keep sexual energy alive is to give full rein to the imagination. Men's ideas and experiments may tend toward the physical, while women's ideas may be more sensual. A woman can use her sensitivity of smell, taste, and touch to help heighten her partner's senses, just as a man can use his bodily awareness to help her feel more sexual. A woman, for example, may introduce music, scents, massage, food, lighting, and fabrics to set a mood, while a man may help her find greater physical pleasure.

In *The New Male Sexuality,* Zilbergeld writes:

> Good sex is not about using any particular organ, following any particular script, or doing any particular act. Rather, it has to do with the emotions generated by whatever you and your partner do. The best definition I've heard derives from an idea of San Francisco sex therapist Carol Ellison and goes like this: "You're having good sex if you feel good about yourself, good about your partner, and good about what you're doing. If later, after you've had time for reflection, you still feel good about yourself, your partner, and what you did, you know you've had good sex." As such, it need not include intercourse or any other specific act or sequence of acts, it need not include orgasm, and the event can take anywhere from a few seconds to several hours.

It will please your partner if you are open to new experiences and sexual styles. When he makes an effort to please you by creating a romantic atmosphere or spending time on foreplay, for example, then you should try to be ready to give him the spontaneous sex that he requests. This flexibility allows you both to enjoy sex without expectations.

In sexual matters, there is a wide range of human experiences, preferences, and desires. It's up to you and your partner to determine together what is best for you both.

Revisit the Best of Times

If your sex life has become routine and boring, you might want to think back on the best sex that you and your partner ever had. What made it so good? Are there any aspects of such episodes that you can recreate?

If the excitement came from being in a new relationship, you might want to change some of the ways you now make love in order to bring novelty back to your sexual relations.

Start over by means of a little role-playing. Act out a first meeting. Go separately to a new place—a coffeehouse or bar or other spot where people meet. Notice each other. Introduce yourselves as different people. Say nothing about your real lives. Flirt. Seduce your partner, or let him seduce you. Try a few sexual moves you've never tried before. Remain open to suggestion. And watch the sparks fly anew.

Another way to play the game is to re-create a first date. Change your names and identities, invite your partner out (under his new identity), and have a date entirely out of your imaginations. Get to know the other's alias. Follow through on the character all the way to the bedroom, if that's where the encounter takes you. Leave your old self behind and enter your exciting new self. Tap into the energy of this new experience. Your desires may have changed since your earlier dating period, and this is a good way to find out.

Play

Watch babies. They are so open and vulnerable. They suck their toes, they laugh when you touch their skin, they smile when you pick them up, and they let you know when they're *not* pleased as well.

If you and your partner are both willing to be open and vulnerable, you can get some of that freedom back through sex. This means letting go of judgment, criticism, and expectations. As Zilbergeld puts it:

> Couples who have good sex over time are adventurous in a child-like way. They play at exploring their own and each other's sensitivities, and they are willing to try out new things, although I hasten to add that this does not mean they try out every new fad that comes along. It's not so much how many different activities and positions they try, but their attitude as they do whatever they do. Many new things don't work—it isn't really that easy, after all, to have intercourse in the bathroom of a 747 or even to get two people into that tiny space—but they have fun finding this out. They have a healthy sense of humor about the whole business. . . . Playing at sex also means not having rigid rules about it, being tolerant for what it is and what it can give. These couples really do take sex any way they can get it rather than having to have it a certain way.

One way to bring play into the bedroom is to try a little game. Take turns being in charge. When your partner is in charge, he asks you to do what he wants. This allows him to become more vulnerable and therefore more open to an intimate relationship with you (something difficult for many men). Then the next time the two of you play this game, you be in charge of what goes on, which will allow you to better express your own sexual desires (something difficult for many women). The aim is to open up to each other. But there's one absolute rule: Each of you has the right to say no to anything you don't want to do. If you practice this over time, it can bring new trust and intimacy to your relationship, deepening and enhancing sexual pleasure for both of you.

Play comes in many forms, as demonstrated by a few survey responses about memorable experiences:

> "Anne left me a voice mail that went something like this: 'Hi, I'm back from Olympia. And all the way home I fantasized about touching every part of your body. Come on over and help me fulfill my fantasy.'"

"When we went camping, and before she got undressed for bed, she laid three sexy little pairs of panties across her sleeping bag and asked which pair I wanted her to try on. She made a fun little game of it, and by the next morning, she had been in and out of all three."

"After making love in the forest in twenty-degree weather, she got up and did jumping jacks."

"She picked me up at the airport wearing only a trench coat, high heels, and that sexy scarf I gave her years ago."

Be New Again

Men love variety. And while you don't have to change the real you that he knows and loves, you can heighten his interest by showing him a few hidden facets of your sexual personality. Be the new lover in the bedroom.

More than 60 percent of men surveyed said that it's important for their partner to "initiate creative sexual encounters" (and the results were even higher—more than 70 percent—for men with children). Yet 65 percent of those who are married and 75 percent of those with children living at home said they aren't getting enough of this.

Do something totally unpredictable. And then do something else the next week or the next month. Keep him on his toes. Play his mistress this week, his master the next. Bring home erotic videos tonight, leave a sweet little love note in the morning. Invite him to meet you at a cheap motel one afternoon and to join you for a picnic in the park on another. Wear ribbons tonight and leather tomorrow.

From one survey respondent: "My partner occasionally dresses in sexy costumes with a fantasy ready to perform when I come home from work."

Pay attention to what he likes best, but don't worry about maintaining an image or setting a precedent. If you've set him up to believe that you're the cute one or the strong one or the responsible one, bring home somebody else: another you. And watch him respond.

Activities to Hone Your Romantic Spirit

- Work with your partner to develop a variety of lovemaking styles. Some may be "quick and dirty"; others may be prolonged and romantic. Negotiate. Take turns. Help your partner to release his sexual imagination and energy.
- Return to the places where you had the most exciting sex, or bring back elements of those situations.
- Flip a coin. The person who wins takes a turn at telling the other exactly what he or she wants sexually. The other simply follows instructions, using no initiative or imagination. The next time you play the game, reverse the roles. But keep in mind that each of you has the right to say "no."
- Invite him on a "sex date." Be a new you.
- Remember to flirt. Try new things. Do away with expectations. Have fun.

Adding Spice

Now that you know the basics, how about a little extra spice for your love life? Surprise your partner with a newfound sense of play, and he'll keep coming back for more. Does this mean romance? Yes!

It goes without saying, however, that anything done in your sexual relationship with your partner is done with respect. Trust and intimacy develop only when you respect your partner, your relationship, and yourself, and seek the same from him.

Share Fantasies

Men and women alike have sexual fantasies. Some of us have been conditioned to feel that such fantasies are unnatural or even "dirty," but they're actually a natural part of the workings of the brain. They are nothing to be embarrassed about or ashamed of. In fact, sharing your fantasies may be a way of bringing new fun into your sex life.

You might not want to reveal your deepest fantasies or even know your partner's. One respondent to the women's survey—who described herself as a petite blond—told of her hurt and disappointment when her husband revealed that his fantasy was seducing a long-legged redhead. Furthermore, if you take a look at *Men in Love* by Nancy Friday, you'll discover that men's fantasies can go far beyond a stimulating sexual encounter with a woman. You would probably consider some of the fantasies presented in that book as downright disgusting.

But you can have fun creating fantasies together, putting both you and your partner in a creative scene. You could start with something as simple as imagining you are complete strangers noticing each other across a crowded room: you approach one another, eyes locked, removing garments as you go, unconcerned about the others who watch, until finally you come together and pull each other's remaining clothes away, and . . . take it from there. Or maybe he's your boss or you're his boss; you've just met at a dance; you're stranded together, naked, after the plane crash in which he saved you. Ham it up.

If this little game gets to be more than you want, let your partner know and try something else, or give it up altogether.

As one survey respondent wrote, "Most fantasies are of a sexual nature rather than a romantic one, but there is a gray area between. Romantic fantasies generally involve some level of role-playing—the romantic pickup, the splurge. Others involve locations, such as a remote, deserted island. Then there are the sexual fantasies. These involve semipublic places for the most part, such as phone booths, taxis, the beach, airplanes, nightclubs. Or they involve other people. But some fantasies are best left in our imagination!"

Practice Massage

Though massage isn't necessarily connected to sex, it's a good way to show your partner that you enjoy touching him and being close. It also helps him become more attuned to his sense of touch as he focuses on his physical responses.

More than 60 percent of men surveyed rated "Give me a massage" as important, and of those men, 65 percent said they aren't getting enough.

When giving your partner a massage, the sensation of your skin touching his will heighten his erotic response if both of you are naked. Try using warm oils so that your hands slide easily over his skin. Let your hair or breasts brush lightly across his back. Add soft kisses, caresses, gentle finger play.

If you are unfamiliar with massage techniques, take a class (your partner might want to join you) or look in your local library or bookstore for a good how-to book.

Bring Home Erotica

Some men find it particularly stimulating when their partner incorporates erotic materials into lovemaking. If this is something you'd like to try, you might buy or borrow books of erotic poetry or stories to read to each other in bed. Or pick up an erotic film to watch.

Increasingly, even mainstream films include erotic scenes. But make sure that you're not getting in over your head by choosing something that may embarrass you or your partner. If you're unsure, you may want to refer to a video review guide at your local library or bookstore, or maybe at the video rental store itself.

Another option is to watch yourselves making love. Many men are turned on by glimpsing their lovemaking in a mirror. Some couples even make videotapes of their lovemaking and find it arousing to watch later (just keep them out of reach of children or anyone else living with you).

You can purchase all sorts of little sex toys these days to add fun to your lovemaking. You're sure to find some of these things vulgar, but others may make you smile—a "whip" made out of soft ribbons, a peacock feather, massage oils, perhaps some very naughty undies. Erotica encompasses anything that will arouse.

If there isn't a store in your area that offers such things, or if you wouldn't be caught dead in one even if there were, try sending away for a catalog. Good Vibrations, a store in San Francisco that features erotica, offers a catalog of its merchandise, which includes books, films, lingerie, sex paraphernalia, and the like, as well as reviews of erotic films. Call 800/289-8423 to order a copy.

Talk Dirty

Now this is one kind of talking that some men would actually like to hear. But it certainly isn't for everyone. It may not fit into your comfort zone, and your partner may consider it vulgar or even think less of you for using such language. So proceed with caution.

Some men in the survey told of their added excitement when their partners used hard-core sex talk in the midst of lovemaking to say what they were going to do or to ask the man to do something to them.

One man told of his delight when his partner cast one of their sexual encounters into a fantasy of "the perfect fuck." This added fun and excitement for both of them. Though he and his partner knew this was a game, and they sometimes broke out laughing in the middle of it, both of them got involved and played along.

You don't have to reserve this talk for the bedroom. If your partner has completely private voice mail, you could leave an enticing message in your sexiest voice.

If you are interested in adding a little verbal fun but embarrassed about using the words, take a look at some cheap romance novels or sex movies on the sly. Take notes; then write your own script and practice. When you know you're alone, say the words aloud. Talking dirty could add a whole new dimension to your sex life. But be prepared for your partner to talk back.

Activities to Hone Your Romantic Spirit

- The next time your partner initiates sex when everything isn't perfect for you, try using some of your favorite techniques to put yourself into the mood and accept his advances anyway. Otherwise you may miss some terrific opportunities to please your partner—as well as yourself.
- In the middle of lovemaking, start whispering a fantasy to your partner that you think might work for you both. He may not get into it the first time, but it should excite his imagination, and he just may be the one who starts it up the next time.
- If you don't know how to give a massage, pick up a good book on the topic or take a class. Maybe your partner will want to learn with you.
- Plan a little afternoon delight. Invite him to play hooky from work one afternoon, or call him in the middle of the day to meet you at home. Have the bedroom set up for a romantic interlude.
- Pick up an erotic (not pornographic) video, and bring it home tonight.
- If there's a quality store in your area that deals in erotica (not pornography), walk in, look around, and see whether there's anything that might add some excitement to your lovemaking. If your area doesn't have an appropriate store (or if you'd rather not show your face there), call Good Vibrations at 800/289-8423 and ask for a copy of its catalog.
- Pick up a trashy romance novel in the grocery store. Give it a quick read. Focus on the most sensuous come-ons and the most vociferous comings. Practice saying the words aloud when you're alone. The next time you're with your partner, use whatever you dare.
- Rent a video that shows how to do a striptease. Get yourself some sexy lingerie and a pair of high heels and long gloves. Practice to your favorite music when you're alone.

When you feel comfortable with it, choose a time when
you know your partner will be receptive, and just do it.

- Do something outrageous: Greet him at the door in your
sexiest lingerie. Bring a can of whipped cream to bed.
Hide from him and leave a trail of clues (pieces of clothing you've shed?), so that by the time he finds you he's
ready too. Use your imagination!

5

Making Occasions Special

Survey respondents expressed delight in receiving romantic gifts from their partners. But what gifts do men consider romantic?

If a man really wants or needs something that's available from a store—and he can afford it—he'll go out and buy it for himself. So, when it comes to gifts for him, that leaves you without a clue, right? Not at all.

According to survey respondents, there are lots of ways to please a man on a special occasion—or any day, for that matter.

The romantic gifts that men want most are those that they cannot buy. To please your own partner, you must know his particular desires. But in the meantime, take a look at how men across the country rated a variety of gift ideas as well as the occasions they consider special.

Giving Gifts of Romance

For starters, men showed little enthusiasm for gifts that relate to their careers. Neither did they get excited about receiving jewelry, music, things for their cars, or gift certificates.

They had moderate interest in games, flowers, books, and magazines. These may be good choices for surprises to give your partner for no special reason, but they probably won't make big hits on his birthday.

So what do men want? Here are the gifts that carry big appeal.

Special Time with You

More than anything else, men want romantic time alone with their partner. The two "gifts" that received the highest ratings were "romantic evenings together (in or out)" and "romantic weekends together (home or away)." In fact, more than 75 percent of men surveyed rated such romantic times as the most desirable gifts.

A romantic escape would make a terrific gift for your partner's birthday. A special dinner would be a great way to thank him for doing something particularly special for you.

You could give your partner an invitation ahead of time, or you could simply surprise him on the occasion itself. The gift could be a wonderful dinner out or a romantic dinner for two at home. It could be a night in the city or a weekend in the country. Or it could be a special time at a locale where you can play together—lolling on the beach, playing tennis, or camping in the woods—whatever you both enjoy doing.

To make it truly romantic, find out what your partner wants. Make all the arrangements. And unless you're just arranging for an evening out, let him know in advance to at least leave time in his schedule.

The focus, of course, should be on having fun with him. This isn't a time for classes or projects or solving problems. And it's important not to be interrupted, so if you have children or others living with you, get a baby-sitter or other help and get away from home.

Make all reservations for your romantic getaway well in advance. When you're at that lakeside cabin in the middle of nowhere, you don't want to learn that the only restaurant for fifty miles can't seat you for dinner until ten o'clock.

If you feel confident that you can pack appropriately for your partner, you can make a night or weekend away a real surprise. Men, however, don't generally value surprises as much as women do, so your best bet may be to give your partner an invitation for the romantic time, and then let him pack for himself. Let him know how long you plan to be away and what sort of equipment he needs to bring (e.g., his bicycle, his snorkeling gear, his swimming trunks). You don't have to divulge the whole story.

In order to satisfy your partner's fantasy, special time away should involve many of the sensual delights that he enjoys. You know him best. But you might want to include some of these:

- Food. Prepare a meal of sensual delights at home, take him to a romantic restaurant, or have a terrific dinner catered at your home or at some exotic setting. Feed him morsels from your plate. You might prepare some choice nibbles—cheese and sliced fruit, sweet strawberries and good champagne—for the bedroom scene. If your plans involve driving to a restaurant in another city, consider either hiring a limousine or taxi to take you both home or making reservations at a nearby hotel or motel.

- Atmosphere. Low lighting is romantic. Candlelight and firelight bring out your best coloring. A picnic on the beach at sunset or in the backyard in the moonlight can be very romantic if thoughtfully planned (just make sure you have privacy). Scents—from perfume, scented candles, massage oils—can add to the atmosphere, as long as they are ones that he likes.

- Clothing. Wear something alluring, something you know he finds attractive on you, something that makes you feel flirty. Layers might be nice: peel them off one by one as the night progresses, or strip down to the sweet little lingerie in one sexy dance. A survey respondent wrote of his excitement when he came home to find his wife in a lacy maid's apron with nothing underneath but garter belt, stockings, and thong panties. If this isn't you, don't try it. But if you would enjoy it, you might also find it's just what he's been wanting.

- Focus. Forget yourself and everything you've done in your life. On your romantic escape, focus on your partner. If he wants to talk, listen without judging or giving advice. If he talks about things or problems that bore you, gently shift the conversation to the moment, to the sensual, to the two of you. Talk about the food, the music, the atmosphere. Talk about how great he looks, smells, and feels. Sit in the quiet with him. Be close. Ask for nothing.

- Play. Make the evening fun—or maybe downright naughty. He's sure to love it. One possible game would be a hunt for jigsaw puzzle pieces that reveal the evening's menu or the night's "entertainment" or that tell him where to find a little gift—or where to find you (buy a blank puzzle and then write or draw something on the pieces). Or plan a role-playing evening during which you'll act out one of his fantasies. Erotic films, stories, or paraphernalia could add to the fun. Or you might just leave a trail of sexy clothing for him to follow when he arrives home (in this case, plan a meal that can wait).

- Privacy. If you go out, make sure that you won't have to rush home. If you're staying in, make sure that no one will arrive in the middle of the "main course." Your partner will appreciate having the entire night alone with you. Mothers must plan ahead: if you're going out, have the baby-sitter arrive in time to take care of the children while you get ready; if you're planning a quiet evening at home, make sure the kids are either fully occupied or at friends' houses long before your plan goes into action.

- Planning. If you need time to become relaxed and sensual, be sure to make that preparation part of your schedule. The last thing you want is for your partner to find you frantic. Cleaning the house, preparing the meal, setting up for the fun, and then getting yourself ready could take a lot of time. Arrange for any help you need in advance. His special evening will be spoiled if you're an emotional wreck or if you complain about all you had to do beforehand. Allow time to bathe slowly, dress slowly, make yourself as sexy as you dare. Remember, this is for him. This is what he wants. So give yourself the time and permission to do it right.

One the highest-rated desires on the survey (selected by more than 90 percent of all respondents) was for partners to be "fun to be around." Here's your chance to shine. Focus on his fantasy. This is the number one gift—the one he can't buy for himself. And he'll love you for it.

Love Notes

Among preferred gifts, running a close second to special time with you, is the love note. Your partner would likely delight in having your love for him spelled out in writing, maybe even framed.

This doesn't mean that you need to take a poetry-writing course. Instead, just put your feelings of love for your partner into words. Use the most intimate terms that you dare. Let him know how much you appreciate him, how much you have enjoyed special times with him, and how you are looking forward to being with him again.

Although it can be a great accompaniment to another gift, a love note is a wonderful little gift by itself anytime. Don't wait for a special occasion. Write it now.

Love notes can be sent to his place of work (with "personal" scrawled across the envelope), they can be sent to his home (even if you share a mailbox), and they can even be written on those little yellow "stickies" and left on his shaving mirror, coffee mug, dashboard, or computer screen.

If you can reach his computer electronically from your own, send him love notes on-line.

If you have a pet name for him, or if he has one for you, be sure to use it. A few examples:

My Darling Teddy,
Miss my big teddy bear . . . longing just to hug him again . . .
makes me feel so safe.
Until then, hope he's thinking of me.
Love & XXX . . .
    Goldilocks

Dearest Michael Michelangelo,
These days without your touch feel cold like marble.

I await the hands that mold me to your own creative wish,
the breath that awakens my sleeping passions,
the kiss that arouses me to your own sweet desires.
Until then, I hold your image in my heart. . . .
        The keeper of your dreams

Leonard Lover,
I have upon my memory such a dream
So sweet, and it was you last night,
But what you made me feel is not for words,
For words alone say only I love you,
And what you are is so much more,
With you I've touched the moon. . . .
Tonight it's full.
I'll meet you there.
        Sylvia

Hey Sam,
I'll be thinking of you all day. You do that to me!
        Later, Shirley

It's best to use your own words, although romantic quotations can be nice as well. In either case, it's not difficult to give your partner something he will cherish. Even a quickly scrawled note can carry great meaning. Writing it down shows that you are willing to formalize your love and appreciation for him. And that's romantic.

A nice card, blank inside, is a fine place to set down your feelings, perfumed stationery adds a special touch, but a scrap of paper will do in a pinch. The thought is what counts. Write it out. Do it now. And watch him smile.

Coupons for Special Favors

Men love being served. To do this for your partner without feeling like the suffering servant, give him a "coupon" (or a book of coupons) and let him know what you are willing to do for him whenever he wants to redeem one. He'll get his service while you stay in control. Make sure he knows that each coupon can be used only once (throw it away after you accomplish the task).

A book of coupons makes a great anniversary gift. And individual coupons are terrific rewards for the special things he does for you. Consider presenting him with coupons offering some of these services:

- Rub your back.
- Rub your feet.
- Massage you all over.
- Prepare and serve your favorite meal.
- Relieve you of one chore today.
- Wash your car.
- Polish your shoes.
- Prepare dinner for your friends.
- Accompany you to a sports event.
- Input your report on the computer.
- Spend an hour with you without talking.
- Take you out to dinner.
- Have sex your way [refer to something specific that he's been wanting and you're willing to do].

If you can discover what he wants and answer his inner desires, he'll feel that he's in control.

If you're concerned that your partner may cash in a coupon at a time that's inconvenient for you, then specify times when you can accept coupons so he won't be disappointed. For example, you might say that coupons are good on weekends only or on Thursday evenings or between five and nine o'clock any evening. Also, specify services that need advance notice, such as the dinner preparation.

To hit the jackpot with this gift, smile while you're pleasing him. Then you're really fun to be around.

Your Own Creations

A man delights in things that his partner creates especially for him. The most common gift of this type is a creation from the kitchen. Special meals, featuring dishes that he particularly enjoys, bring him pleasure and let him know that you truly care. You win extra points if you create a special dish for him that no one else knows how to make. But first, of course, you need to know his preferences.

- If he has praised a certain dish at a restaurant, for example, try your hand at making it (some restaurants are willing to give out their recipes).
- If you have another creative talent that your partner truly appreciates, use it to give him special attention.
- If he likes your painting or drawing, present him with a work you made especially for him. You might even frame it for his work space.
- If you write well, besides sending love notes and love letters, you might compose a poem or even a story about the two of you (perhaps engaging in his fantasy).
- If you make quilts, make one for him. If you sew, make him an item of clothing he will enjoy.
- If your medium is wood, metal, or clay, craft something that will make him smile.
- If you play a musical instrument, play something special just for him. If you create your own music, compose a piece for him.
- If you're a dancer, dance for him.
- If you have a lovely voice, sing for him. Or find something beguiling to read to him.
- If you have a knack for interior design, create a special room for the two of you to enjoy together.
- If you're a gardener, bring him your vegetables or your flowers.
- And if you feel sexy, show it, for that can be a creative gift, too.

From one survey respondent: "She wrote a song about us and sang it to me. She's not a songwriter, and she's very shy about performing. So I not only felt her trust in me, but I also felt very special."

Your own talent is the most personal gift you can give— something he can't buy, something no one else could possibly give him. So turn your talent toward the man you love. It not only reaffirms your uniqueness, but it also lets him know that you think he is worthy of the time and effort you put into the production of such a gift. Remember, men express their love through doing, so your partner will particularly appreciate the fact that you are doing something for him.

Mementos of Your Time Together

Though many men would rather not be called sentimental, they do treasure mementos of times spent with their partners. These may include photographs of the two of you, little souvenirs you picked up on your travels, or a scrapbook of postcards, ticket stubs, and other items that evoke memories. Such gifts are especially appropriate for your anniversary, when you celebrate your time together. Know your partner and you'll know how much he'll cherish different kinds of mementos.

A framed photograph of the two of you makes an especially nice gift for his place of work. This is a surprise that you can give him anytime. Try sneaking it into his office or work space and putting it on his desk or hanging it on the wall while he's away on a business trip or out to lunch.

Fathers appreciate receiving photographs of their children as well as of the whole family. This is a wonderful gift for Father's Day. If the children are young, a new photo at least once a year will please your partner. If he's the camera buff, select a slide or negative of a photo that he took himself, have it enlarged, and put it into an attractive desktop frame.

While you're at it, he would also like a photo of you alone. This can be a photo that he took when you were on vacation together or a photo that you commission to be taken professionally. If you go the professional route, don't be shy about arranging for a special mood that you would like the picture to evoke. If you dare, locate a photography service that takes provocative portraits. Some will do your hair and makeup as well as supply costumes and sets; all you have to do is show up, and you'll look great.

Gifts that evoke special times together can also be romantic. A few survey respondents wrote about gifts from their partners that related to special times they had shared. One example: "My lovelady and I go to coffeehouses together whenever we can, so when she brought me an espresso machine, it was great, because now we can enjoy our cappuccinos right at home as well. It has added a special touch particularly to our Sunday mornings on the back porch, where we relax together with the cat and the newspaper."

Clothes and Shopping Together

It might surprise you to know that more than half the men surveyed would like to receive clothing as a gift. In order to shop for your partner's clothing, however, you must know his preferences as well as his sizes. Some men were distressed when they felt their partner was trying to change their style. "I don't like wearing purple," one man wrote, "but my wife likes purple so she keeps getting me shirts and ties and even socks that have purple in them." Unless your partner has asked for a makeover, match colors and styles to the clothes he already wears. Men don't want their partners to try to change them.

A way to make this fun for both of you—and to make sure he gets the clothes he wants—is to give your partner an invitation to spend time with his "personal shopper." Specify the item or items for which you offer to shop with him (e.g., a shirt and tie, a pair of shoes, or a suit).

Don't hand him a gift certificate from a store and expect him to go out shopping for himself; this is definitely not romantic. Besides, you don't want to put a dollar amount on your gift lest it appear to be a check, which would be even less romantic.

The invitation should specify the gift as well as the fact that you plan to spend time with him shopping for it. You may want to put down a date and time (e.g., Saturday morning at ten) to give this outing the commitment it deserves.

Adding a brunch, luncheon, or cozy dinner to your personal shopping spree is a nice touch.

Small Surprises

Men delight in receiving little surprises for no reason—almost as much as women do. More than 60 percent of the men surveyed rated such gifts as desirable.

A fun way to give such a gift is to hide it in a place where your partner is sure to find it. To know precisely what to give him, you have to know his interests, tastes, and desires. But here are some possibilities:

- Nearly half the men surveyed rated "hobby or sporting equipment" as a desirable gift. So if your partner has a favorite activity, give him something he's sure to use. Keep in mind that the brand name may be important here. Perhaps he'd like golf balls (buy a pack of his preferred brand and have the balls engraved with his initials); sport socks (with a love message printed on them); a set of bicycle tools or a water bottle; a fun hat, visor, or headband; a waterproof parka; a piece of rock-climbing gear; a good pair of gardening gloves; or a case for displaying his coin collection. If he belongs to a gym or sports club, check out its special offerings (e.g., racquetball classes or professional massage).
- If he follows a local sports team on TV, buy a couple of tickets and accompany him to a game. If you don't enjoy this sort of outing, get tickets for your partner to go with the children or one of his friends.
- If he enjoys board games, computer games, or puzzles, check out your local game or computer store to see what might engage him.
- If he likes to snack, leave his favorite food in the cupboard or refrigerator for him to find when he has the munchies. Add a brief love note, and you've made it special.

- If he's an avid reader, pay attention to his reading choices. Browse your local bookstore to find good books on his favorite subjects or those written by his favorite authors. The next time you're in a bookstore together, see what catches his eye.
- Is the garage his haven? You could fill his toolbox with items from his favorite supplier. But be advised that tools are often specialized and choices can be personal. If you don't know the exact tool in the exact size by the exact manufacturer that he wants, this may be a good item for a coupon (e.g., "good for one set of wrenches") in which you offer to shop with him.
- Does he have a favorite cartoonist, or does he enjoy doing crossword puzzles or playing other pencil games? You can probably find booklets filled with such distractions among the magazines at your local grocery or drugstore.
- If he enjoys flowers, pick or send him a bouquet.
- What kind of erotica pleases him? Literature, films, ostrich feathers? Among his favorite things will be the sexy garments you wear to show off your body.
- Surprise him with love notes anytime, anywhere. Put them in the mail, in his gym bag, in his medicine cabinet, in his briefcase . . . and he'll be thinking of you.

Pay attention to his reactions to your gifts so you'll learn how to please him even more. The key is to listen with your heart, and then surprise him with your insight. Your new-found knowledge will help you to make any day special. And that's romantic.

Celebrating His Favorite Occasions

Judging from the way some men act, you might think they don't care to celebrate anything. But the men who responded to the survey did rate some days as special and important.

Your Anniversary

At the top of most men's list is their anniversary. For you and your partner, this may mean the day the two of you met, a special day that you both remember as the beginning of your relationship, or the day you got married.

If your partner isn't in the habit of planning something nice, such as an evening out, for this day, you could take the initiative by suggesting that the two of you work on a plan together: "Our anniversary is coming up. Let's plan something fun." This could be as simple as a romantic dinner you prepare together. But whether you stay home or go out, this day is just for the two of you; it's not a time to invite friends along.

Unless you're already in the habit of giving your partner a gift on this day, he probably doesn't expect one. But a little love note is certainly appropriate—and an opportunity to express your appreciation for your relationship with him.

His Birthday

A man values his birthday because it's the one day he can call his own. When you celebrate this day with him, you are celebrating his very existence. This is the day to give him that special gift he wants. It's a day to surprise him by making or treating him to a dinner he'll savor.

If you have children, get them involved in Dad's birthday. Depending on how old they are, they may be able to help wrap and present gifts, assist you in the kitchen, blow up balloons, or put candles on the cake. Take advantage of the fact that children love birthday parties.

Although surprise parties didn't earn high ratings on the gift list, a number of men wrote about a surprise their wife or girlfriend gave them to recognize a birthday milestone. The favorites were surprise getaways. Some examples:

"On my fortieth birthday, my wife 'kidnapped' me. She arranged a weekend at a bed-and-breakfast on the coast. She brought along a picnic basket with wine, fruit, and snacks for our arrival. That evening, she took me to dinner at an outstanding restaurant and scheduled a long massage after dinner. The B and B had a private hot tub that guests could reserve by the hour, which stood on a deck overlooking the ocean, and we took advantage of that. The next day we drove to the nearby arty town and then drove down the coast and through the redwood forest. I felt particularly special because she's a busy, career-minded professional. It showed me how much she cares for me and our relationship."

"On my thirtieth birthday, my girlfriend had a limousine pick us up, and she told me that the evening was all mine to do whatever I wanted. Of course, she had a few backup ideas up her own sleeve . . . and we both had a terrific time."

"When I turned forty, I arrived at my office to find that my wife had come in the previous evening and decorated it for me. And when I arrived home, she was sitting on the couch in her lingerie with a bottle of champagne and a birthday cake she had made, and she had a great dinner ready to throw into the oven—whenever we were ready."

"My lovelady had a surprise birthday party for me and asked me to marry her. I had been trying to get *her* to say yes for months."

Father's Day

If your partner is a dad, Father's Day matters to him. Because it always falls on a Sunday, this is a good day to free him from household chores and let him just relax, whether at home or playing his favorite sport somewhere else.

Unless your children are very small, they should take a large role in helping serve Dad on his special day and in helping you with any plans.

You may want to make your partner's favorite dinner on Father's Day. And it's appropriate for the children to present him with a gift. He will particularly cherish something they made for him, such as a drawing he can hang on his wall or bulletin board at work.

By the way, here's a peek into fathers' hearts: fathers who answered the survey rated "the children's birthday" as the most important celebration for them—above even their own birthday.

Christmas or Hanukkah

About 60 percent of survey respondents rated Christmas or Hanukkah as important to them, and more than 70 percent of those with children in the household felt this way. These men enjoy the family quality of the winter holidays, which may recall boyhood days full of surprise and delight. The annual celebrations can evoke much nostalgia, fostered by memories of a warm and cozy home, gathering around a fire, putting lights on a tree, caroling, participating in religious services, sharing with friends and family.

Unfortunately, the holidays may be a stressful time for you. Women are typically the ones expected to shop for gifts, prepare food, and make nice with the relatives. If your partner is one of those men who enjoys the holidays, you might want to encourage him to get more involved with the planning and the festivities.

Looking at the other side, however, about 40 percent of survey respondents did not rate these holidays as important. To know how to please your partner during the holidays, be sure you find out what he enjoys.

Thanksgiving

A holiday that wasn't listed on the survey but that some men actually added is Thanksgiving. This is a cozy day for the family to spend together at home. It's also a great time for you to give thanks for your relationship and create your own family traditions.

Valentine's Day

Less than half the men surveyed rated Valentine's Day as important to them. For one thing, as a commercial holiday, it lacks the unique quality of an individual's birthday or a couple's anniversary.

Even so, because it celebrates romance, Valentine's Day is a good time to remind your partner of the love you have for him. A love note is a fine way to do this.

New Year's Eve

New Year's Eve wasn't listed on the survey, but some men added it as an occasion they enjoy. Whether you and your partner celebrate at home or on the town, alone or with friends, this may be a good opportunity to put any differences behind you and start anew—with fresh understanding and appreciation for one another.

And on your list of resolutions for the new year, be sure to include a lot of romance.

Your Private Holiday

You can also create your own holiday—a ritual that may become important to your relationship.

In responding to the survey, a few men wrote about annual trips or outings they take with their partner (sometimes including other special friends) to a particular place at a particular time of year. This personal holiday might be a ski trip, a camping trip, or a trip to the city where the couple met. For some, it took place on a birthday, Thanksgiving, or an anniversary, but for others it was simply a fun outing they could look forward to each year. As one man wrote, "It builds continuity in the relationship."

Occasions Important to You

In spite of their interest in celebrating special occasions, men have been known to overlook important dates, including their own anniversaries and their partner's birthdays. Many men seem to forget key dates from one year to the next. One survey respondent, who had frequently disappointed his wife by forgetting important dates, was pleased that she took the initiative every January to write "Billy's birthday," "our anniversary," and so forth on the appropriate days in his new calendar.

Remember that your partner doesn't want to disappoint you. If he doesn't keep a calendar or if you don't have access to it, don't be shy about reminding him of your anniversary—or any other date that matters to you.

Activities to Hone Your Romantic Spirit

- Plan a special night or weekend together, either at home or away. Send him an invitation in the mail far enough in advance so that he'll be prepared.
- Get in the habit of leaving little love notes around for your partner to find. Surprise him with variety—from self-stick notes on his shaving mirror to handwritten messages on nice stationery or cards sent through the mail.
- Which holiday celebrations are important to your partner? If you don't already know, ask him. Then make plans.
- What material things does your partner talk about wanting? Are they things you can afford? If so, consider wrapping them up for his birthday or the holidays. If you don't have a clue as to what he wants or what would please him, watch where he shops, check out the magazines he reads, or ask his friends. You can also ask him directly, but do it months ahead of the time you plan to give him the gift, so that he won't expect it.
- How does your partner enjoy spending his free time? If it involves tools or equipment, visit a store or clubhouse that specializes in his sport or hobby. There you can check out the opportunities for small surprise gifts and talk with other enthusiasts to find out which items your partner might particularly appreciate.
- If your partner sometimes forgets days that are special to you, offer to mark them in his calendar.

6

Managing Time . . . Reaching Goals

Unlike most men, women often have to juggle more than one type of work. Men can typically focus their most productive time and energy on one career. Women, however, are not only pursuing careers outside the home, they are also generally responsible for ensuring the smooth running of the household itself along with the welfare of those living in it. At the same time, many women take on the added responsibility of caring for a sick or elderly relative.

Both men and women surveyed said that one of the biggest constraints on romance is lack of time. There are so many obligations, and everyone is just plain worn out. So how can you find the time, let alone the energy, to be romantic?

The buildup of minor resentments concerning household chores and family responsibilities can deaden any relationship. To avoid this, you must communicate regularly with your partner about feelings regarding this issue. Unless you do, such resentments will surely interfere with romance.

As one man wrote, "Our relationship would be more romantic if she would learn to relax and unwind and deal better with stress. The major stress in my life is just dealing with seeing her stressed out with parenting and her career. If she were happier with herself, it would go a long way to opening up romance in our relationship."

If You're a Mom

If you have children of any age living at home—whether you spend your days at work outside the home and then return to the kids or whether you spend your days with the youngsters—you are probably physically and emotionally stretched, stressed, and exhausted. Mothers must give seemingly infinite amounts of time, energy, and emotional support.

Women who answered the survey for the book *How to Romance the Woman You Love—The Way She Wants You To!* revealed that the responsibility of caring for children affects romance more than anything else. Unfortunately, it usually affects romance in a negative way. A major complaint of mothers is the loss of control over their time. Women generally change their personal schedules and give up lots of free time in order to care for children. And at some level, many women resent this loss of freedom. Furthermore, because children's needs can't be scheduled or postponed, women who have been terrific time managers in the office are often at loose ends when it comes to coping with the demands of child-rearing.

Moreover, mothers often feel resentful when their partners don't contribute a fair share. Even if domestic responsibilities were split fifty-fifty before any children entered the scene, it is the mother who invariably shoulders the added duties that come with the arrival of a baby. Sure, a good dad might diaper or feed the baby once in a while, play with the growing child, or help the little scholar with her homework, but it's the mother who holds ultimate responsibility here. All too often, the father can choose when to participate.

Most men can set up their lives to limit interruptions. But for Mom, having children means endless interruptions. Mothers who don't have a well-planned strategy for handling this situation may take on the entire burden, quietly but unhappily enduring in the role of suffering servant. Such women periodically come unglued in one way or another, sometimes blowing up at their startled partner or even the children

According to Dr. Gerald Smith, although a mother may think she is doing the best for her children if she quietly endures, the role of suffering servant actually gives children a terrible role model. If children view their mother as a tireless worker who doesn't consider herself worthy of her own time, it can lower the children's self-esteem. Instead, youngsters need to see their mother's enlightened self-interest: "I'll finish this for myself and then help you in a minute."

You may be thinking of waiting it out—"as soon as the baby learns to sleep through the night" or "once he gets past these terrible twos" or "in a few more years, when she leaves for college." Don't count on it. Though a child's needs change as the years go by, the needs do continue. In the meantime, your relationship with your partner is suffering. Do you want to spend that many years without romance? Will there be any romance left once the children have left home?

Waiting for the situation to improve itself only causes resentment. Have you ever blown up at your partner because he wasn't doing his fair share? Men have expressed their frustration, guilt, and even feelings of helplessness when their partner points out everything she must cope with in order to care for home and family. Men actually do want to help, but all too often they don't know how. In fact, they frequently feel excluded from the nurturing role: Mother has her own way of doing things and she doesn't want interference. Generally, the woman makes the decisions about what her partner should and shouldn't do to help; to make matters worse, she often micromanages his efforts ("Don't hold the baby that way!"). What's a guy to do?

According to Dr. Bernie Zilbergeld:

Because of the heavy pummeling they have received from women in their lives, from the media, and from therapists, many men are resentful and despairing. Whatever they do and everything they are is somehow wrong, bad, or inadequate. They believe they are willing to change, but it seems that they can't quite understand what is wanted of them or can't make the changes fast enough or can't make enough of them. The withdrawal by men that many women complain of is often no more than the manifestation of the men's just giving up. They can't deal with hearing of more things they are doing wrong, more ways in which they are incompetent. While this withdrawal hurts women, it also hurts men in a profound way because they know full well that withdrawal from conflict is itself the antithesis of what they've been taught about masculinity.

This situation affects the whole family. A woman can become so invested in the nurturing process that it comes out as controlling. Then the father becomes what appears to be a second-class parent, and the kids pick up on that. It's not good for the children, and it can damage the relationship between the parents.

It would be better for Mom to accept the way that Dad parents. The fact that he does things differently is actually an advantage for the children because they learn to adapt to different styles. This is useful preparation for life, which requires so much flexibility these days.

Moreover, children whose parents show love for each other will have a much better chance of developing meaningful love relationships as adults. You can provide your children with a good example by letting your love for your partner flourish. Instead of waiting, enjoy life in the present. In order to make your romance last into the future, you've got to plan and strategize today.

According to Smith, the parents who succeed at keeping romance in their relationship are those who take time off the top. They schedule quality time for themselves. The couples whose relationships dry up and become subsumed by parenting are those who attempt to connect with each other with what's left over; they share only the dregs of their time.

If you, like most moms, feel constrained by time, energy, and emotional demands, this chapter will help you regain some of the control you once had over your life—and make room for romance. It begins with some basics about time management. Then it shows you how to ask for help by approaching your partner with solutions instead of problems. Finally, this chapter provides tools with which you can set and accomplish your long-term personal goals.

Activities to Hone Your Romantic Spirit

- Make a mental list of everything you're doing for your children, and start giving yourself credit. Think of how you are helping them grow and mature, and congratulate yourself each time one of your children accomplishes something new. Instead of viewing yourself as the suffering servant, see yourself as a counselor, teacher, chef, chauffeur, nurse, friend, and, of course, mother. Value your multifaceted role.
- Imagine that your children are grown and on their own (it happens quicker than you might think) and that you and your partner have time for romance again. How would you like to spend this time with him?
- The next time you and your partner are together in the presence of your children, make a point of showing them the care you and your partner have for each other. Put your hand on his, give him a hug, give him a little kiss. Start enjoying your time together in the present.

Managing Your Time

"Manage my time? That sounds like something for the office," you might say. "I don't have that kind of control over things at home. Things at home can't wait. If Sammy falls down, I can't reschedule the urgent 'meeting' with him to bandage his knee. And I don't have any 'staff' at home to help out. I have to do it all myself."

According to Smith, trying to squeeze time, or compress everything you need to do into a certain amount of time—"time urgency"—generates irritability and impatience. And if you're in a constant state of stress from time urgency, it's unlikely that you will have much energy for romance.

Do you control your time, or does the clock control your time? Do you feel that you have to hit every green light during the day just to make it? At the end of each day, do you feel as though you're still running and yet you haven't accomplished nearly as much as you had planned? If so, read on. You're not alone.

Time managers and efficiency experts have studied corporations in depth to come up with suggestions for changing work habits. And though home life may not involve running a meeting or closing a sale, the basic ideas for managing time to enhance efficiency and ease stress transfer easily from the corporate boardroom to your own family room.

To improve your time-management skills, invest in a pencil and a pad of quadrille paper (the kind with little blue squares all over it). That's all you need. If you have a laptop computer with you at all times, you can use that instead.

If you can manage your time well, you will be able to start relaxing. You will have more time to take care of yourself physically, mentally, and emotionally. You will be able to pursue goals. You will have more time to do virtually nothing, which often begets creativity. All of this will not only open up more time and energy for your love relationship, but it will also help you feel happier with your life and therefore more inclined toward romance.

Monitor Your Time

Where does the time go? It must have been a woman who first said, "The harder I work, the behinder I get." The first step in time management is to find out exactly how you spend your time. Time management experts tell us that 20 percent of the things we do each day yield 80 percent of the results, and 80 percent of our activities yield only 20 percent of the results. With this in mind, it's time to discover where your time goes.

This may seem tedious—a waste of time in itself—but it's a critical starting point. For one week, carry your quadrille pad with you wherever you go. You are going to keep track of time spent, in fifteen-minute intervals. Whenever you begin a task (e.g., get into the car to pick Sally up from band practice, begin to cook dinner, open the mail, carry the laundry to a place where you'll fold it), write down the start time. When you finish the task, write down the finish time.

If you are employed outside the home, mark that time in one daily entry as "job." So, for example, you may begin your day with a number of household items, such as "help Billy get dressed," "make four lunches," and "take Jennifer to day care," before you write "job," which should start when you commence traveling to your place of work and end when you first encounter your family in the evening or when you get into the car to pick up the children from school. However, if you take care of family matters during the day (for example, taking Tommy to a doctor appointment, running errands at noon, or spending time on the phone with Jenny's teacher), include those tasks separately.

Write down everything you do in each twenty-four-hour period during one week, including watching television, relaxing, sleeping, exercising, and doing other things for yourself. Your weekend will probably look different from your weekdays, but it's important to keep track of what you do then as well. If you read in bed until 1:00 A.M. on Saturday night, be sure to write that down. And sex? Well, you might want to use a code there, just so no one who could peek at this learns too much about your private affairs. In any event, for one week, keep your quadrille pad with you at all times.

Once you have your week's record, put it aside in a safe place. You'll need this information later to realign your use of time.

While creating this record, you may already have noticed some things you would like to change. But before you start putting your newfound time into areas that don't pay off, take a look at some of the standard time-wasters.

Eliminate Time-Wasters

You may be able to relieve some time pressure by eliminating some of the time you waste each day. This is not to say that you shouldn't relax. Relaxation time isn't wasted time; it's time for you. Wasted time is time spent inefficiently on a task, where too much time is spent for the desired outcome. You can use your weekly record to help you evaluate the outcome from the time you spend at each task. But there are some standard time-wasters that you can probably change right away. In the end, this will not only give you more time for romance, but it will also add to your peace of mind, which in turn will allow you to adopt a more romantic attitude on a daily basis.

Mail   Do you have a pile of old mail somewhere? This is the stuff that you didn't have to deal with when it arrived, so you put it aside for later. Most of us have a little cleaning up to do in this area. Of course, it will take a little time, but this is the start of something new, which will save you time in the future.

Set aside a few hours to go through the entire mail pile, and dump, dump, dump! Most of what you find will probably be too old to worry about—expired coupons, dated catalogs, old sweepstakes forms, invitations to bygone events. Dump them. The rest will probably be irrelevant. Dump them, too.

File anything that's important enough to keep. If you don't already have a filing system, get yourself a file box and some manila folders. Label them as "Bills," "Paid Bills," "Medical Insurance," "Credit Card Info," "Bank," "Vacation," "Receipts," "PTA," "Income Tax," "Grover Middle School," "Coupons," "Charity," "Maps," and so on. Use labels that correspond with the type of mail that you handle and the records that you want to keep. Keep the file box within easy access, and organize the folders so that they are easy to find (such as alphabetically). This filing system should be purged at least once a year (perhaps at income tax time).

Now that you've eliminated the pile, how do you keep a new one from forming?

Handle each incoming piece of mail two times only: once to file, a second time to batch process. The first time involves opening the envelope and putting the contents into the right folder, or directly into the garbage or recycling bin, or into your partner's in-box if it's something he must deal with. The second time is when you open the file to pay, balance, respond to, or use all the items within. For example, you may open the bills file on a weekly basis, the bank file on a monthly basis, and the coupon file each time you go to the supermarket. Dump the detritus. Piles are distracting. Piles are passé. Piles are not romantic.

Be sure to open the mail each day at a time when you can immediately go through it, read what needs to be read, file what needs to be filed, and dump what needs to be dumped. This means if you arrive home from work carrying a crying baby who requires immediate attention, don't open the mail. Wait until the baby is playing happily or down for the night.

By the way, junk mail is just that, not "junque" to be kept for posterity. This category generally includes catalogs, sales flyers, advertising supplements, and all those other things that you stash for later, just in case. The only thing you can gain from opening a catalog is another bill. Toss it without turning a page. There: you're back in control. And you're already saving lots of time.

Disorganization   If you've ever spent time looking for a particular pen or garden spade or pair of earrings, you may need to organize your surroundings. Time managers call this "mastering your work environment."

What types of things do you need to carry out your responsibilities? If you can put these in an order that's easily maintained, you will reduce the time you spend beginning each task. Moreover, when you have the proper tools at the ready, you will find each task easier to approach so you may actually feel happier while accomplishing it.

Again, the initial organization will take time, so you may want to break it into small parts. You could concentrate on one room a month, doing one section of that room each week. For example, you might tackle the kitchen in February, each week organizing a set of cupboards or drawers. Then do your bedroom in March—closets, drawers, jewelry boxes. In May you might go into the nursery. How about the basement and then the garage?

The key is to organize in a way that allows you to maintain order easily. If other members of the household use the items in a space you're reorganizing, try to enlist their advice and support in the reorganization. After all, if your partner and children are involved in creating the solution, they'll be much more willing to help keep things in place. This could even spell the end of picking up after them.

One way to organize a small part of your daily life is to create a "staging area." Designate a table or shelf near the front door as the place where you will put your keys, your backpack, your briefcase, and anything else that you need to take with you the next time you go out.

Television Perhaps you use TV programs to learn about cooking, to exercise, or to practice yoga. Or maybe you watch educational shows with your youngsters. Or you watch entertaining feature shows in the evening with your partner.

If there is a purpose to your TV viewing—that is, if the value of the outcome at least equals the value of the time put into it—then it may be worthwhile. But if you think that watching sitcoms every evening is the best way to relax with your family, think again.

One way to evaluate time spent watching TV is to decide how it affects your life and your family relationships. After an hour or two in front of the set, do you and your family feel relaxed, do the shows stimulate conversation, or do you all simply feel drugged, wanting the programming to continue so that you won't have to get up from the couch to turn it off? Another way to evaluate TV-viewing is by determining whether you routinely turn on the television no matter what shows are scheduled or whether, instead, you select only the shows of greatest educational, informational, and entertainment value to you.

If your TV-watching falls into the category of habit, try interacting instead. Get a game your family can play together. Go for a walk. Read to one another. Sing and play musical instruments together. Begin a family project that you can work on together each evening. Turn off the television, and quiz Melanie for the spelling bee and help Davey read a book. Some families put the TV on a cart and keep it in the closet, wheeling it out only when special shows air.

Start small by trying to get the whole family involved in something enjoyable just one night a week. But don't despair if they won't budge. Use that time instead to work toward your personal goals (see "Setting Personal Goals" toward the end of this chapter). You'll feel better for it. And they may just come around to find out what's so interesting.

Maybe you have the TV on while you do household chores. Turn it off. Television keeps you from concentrating on completing your work. Listening to the radio is less distracting. You'll finish your housework more quickly and have time for something rewarding, such as playing with your children, planning your next career move, doing some volunteer work, or even romancing your partner.

Communication Systems   Today we have beepers, car phones, electronic mail, answering services—you can't get away from these devices. If someone wants to talk to you, you're there. When a client, friend, associate, or family member says, "You got my message, didn't you?" you have no excuse.

Everyone needs friends, and it's important to keep up with those who contribute to your happiness and well-being, just as it's important to support those who need your help. But if you find yourself regularly gossiping about irrelevant matters or listening to someone who just wants to talk, it's time to cut the cord. If you feel guilty about always being the one who says, "gotta go," try letting your answering machine take your calls. Call back only the friends who aren't behaving as though you have all the time in the world to chat. Because you don't!

Of course, you don't want to lose good friends. If you and your friends enjoy talking on the phone about your days, your children, your problems, then it's important to keep in touch. The key is to examine every relationship that regularly takes up your time and to determine whether that relationship's value equals the value of the time you spend.

Alcohol   For some, feeling frustrated and out of control can lead to alcohol abuse. If you drink on a daily basis, think about how it affects your time. It might be sapping your energy, stealing your evenings, or even coming between you and your family. Alcohol and other drugs can keep you from focusing on the important aspects of life. If you cannot control certain aspects of your time because of alcohol or drug use, you probably need to get outside help.

Keeping Track

Take a look at your weeklong record of spent time and try to identify anything that's taking you longer than it should. How can you do it more efficiently? Some tasks are more efficiently handled in a batch because of setup and teardown time. Examples are paying bills, doing loads of laundry, and running a series of errands. Other activities, such as organizing everything in your home, are better broken into steps, because trying to accomplish them all at once would overwhelm you.

Also identify any activity on your record that is simply a waste of your time. Make a list of all your time-wasters, and next to each item jot down how you plan to modify or eliminate it. Is it important to spend time sorting coupons, for example? Unless you really need them, toss them. You can be very efficient at doing irrelevant tasks, but that does not make you effective.

Refer frequently to your list. It may take a while to break a habit, but if you do, you'll reap great benefits over time.

Grow Your Effectiveness

Besides the things that are simply wasting your time, there are sure to be things in your weekly record that do require your time but that aren't as important as other activities. One way to cut back on low-priority work is to do it less frequently.

A good example is housework. You could easily spend a whole week doing only housework—washing floors and windows, straightening closets, dusting, vacuuming, cleaning toilets, getting the cobwebs out of the ceiling corners. But what if *right now* you learned that company was coming in one hour? You'd have your place shining by the time the company arrived. The point is, while there will always be rooms that need daily tidying, such as the kitchen and your bedroom, you may be spending more time than is necessary in other areas. Which areas in your home collect the most dirt and clutter? Focus on these areas each day. Others can be batched for a weekly or biweekly cleaning. Some things, such as ovens, windows, and floorboards, may need only monthly or seasonal cleanings. Simply keeping things in the right places, as previously discussed, can go a long way toward reducing cleanup time.

Take a look at other areas of your life. What other low-priority tasks can you do less often? Purchasing a few more pairs of panties might allow you to do fewer loads of laundry. Arranging a car pool with your neighbor might save you half the time you now spend taking the children to school. Weekly meal planning could save you last-minute trips to the grocery store.

Maybe you needn't go to the grocery store at all. Shopping and delivery services are popping up all over the country, and some are accessible through your computer. Check with your local supermarket to see what services it offers.

Banks and other financial institutions are going on-line as well. You can now pay your bills, transfer money from one account to another, and even buy and sell stocks from the comfort of your home or office.

Corresponding by electronic mail can also save time. Through one of the on-line communication systems, your friends and colleagues can send you e-mail from all over the world, and you can answer them when you have the time.

What must you do to give yourself more time? Whatever it is may demand a little setup time to get your started, but you'll end up way ahead.

Prioritize Tasks

To regain control of your time, it's important to replace reaction with "pro-action." In other words, you must anticipate the demands on your time and decide what can and cannot wait, rather than raging or panicking at the innumerable chores that inevitably present themselves.

To eliminate some of the time urgency from your life, start making notes. Take out that quadrille pad again, and go to your weekly record. Put an asterisk on those tasks that *must* be done (on a daily or weekly basis). Now write those tasks on a clean piece of paper. This is your priority list.

On another piece of paper, over the next week or so, generate a list of all those things that aren't getting done because you have no time. These are not your priorities, but they should be done at some point. This list may include your household reorganizations. It may include things that need repair—a dining room chair, a skirt zipper, Tommy's bicycle—whether by you, your partner, or an expert. Maybe you've wanted to shop for something—new drapes, a new car. Even getting your car washed may be eluding you. List everything you would like to accomplish over and above your family priorities. Put an asterisk next to the most significant items—the ones with the greatest urgency or payoff.

Now, on each nonpriority item, put the date you will do the task. If a task is too lengthy to accomplish in an hour or so, break it down into parts. Plan to spend at least an hour each week on one of these items. Meet your deadlines.

As you accomplish items, check them off. And reward yourself for every accomplishment. Add to this list as the weeks go on. When you run out of space on one page, transfer all the things not yet accomplished onto a clean sheet and begin again. If you find that you aren't getting these nonpriority items done as you expected, give yourself more time for each.

By the way, romance is a priority. You want it to be strong and vital long after the children have left home. So give it an asterisk, and do it every day.

Activities to Hone Your Romantic Spirit

• For one week, keep a log of how you spend your time. On a quadrille pad, use a page for each day of the week. On each page, write times of day in fifteen-minute intervals, beginning with midnight and going to midnight. Keep your pad with you at all times. Each time you begin a task, write it down in the appropriate section, and as soon as you complete the task, draw a line from the beginning time to the ending time (i.e., crossing through as many fifteen-minute intervals as it took). If you work outside the home, you can note the time you leave the house for work and then draw a line through to the time you return home. But if you spend time on tasks unrelated to work during the day—exercising at noon, talking to your child's teacher on the phone, lunching with a friend, picking up groceries on the way home—note these separately in your log.

• Imagine that you have only half the total time to spend that you actually have. Then go through your weeklong record, putting an X next to the time-wasters you need to eliminate and a check mark next to tasks you could do more efficiently.

• Make a commitment to get rid of time-wasters. Turn off the TV. Conceive a plan to organize your things and spaces. Become less available to people who waste your time.

• Keep your list of daily priorities in plain view, and don't lose sight of what must be accomplished each day. Let other things fall by the wayside as needed.

• Make a list of nonpriority items you would like to accomplish over the next few months. Break these down into doable tasks and set reasonable deadlines. As you accomplish items, check them off and reward yourself. Add to the list as needed.

• If you find that you are often late for meetings, appointments, and other scheduled commitments, or if your children are repeatedly late for school, take stock of your daily procedures. What can you do to get back in control? Make the choice to control your time rather than letting the clock control it.

• Let everyone who needs to get in touch with you know the best time to reach you during the day.

• In a place where others can see it, post a list of what must be done each day along with directions to important places (Bobby's day care, the doctor's office) and emergency phone numbers. Then, if a problem comes up and you aren't there, others (a neighbor, a baby-sitter, your partner) can easily step in.

• Take a look at all the ways you are managing your time and your family's time. And give yourself some credit.

Delegating Responsibility

While evaluating the time that you spend on daily responsibilities, you may have realized that you're doing quite a bit, maybe more than what you consider to be your fair share. If so, you're probably either playing the silent role of suffering servant or you're openly resentful.

But have you tried delegating? "Sure," you might say. "The last time I complained to my partner, he said, 'Okay, okay,' and he vacuumed the floor, took the baby for a walk, and then went off to play tennis. And I was supposed to be grateful."

Delegating isn't about complaining or nagging. Rather, it's about planning, training, setting deadlines, and sometimes negotiating. It can even involve a series of irresistible incentives.

You've got to distribute the responsibilities, set deadlines, and follow up. You and your delegatees have to agree on tasks far in advance of when they need to be done so that you won't be dropping something on someone at the last minute. You may even have to train someone who's new to a task. As with other aspects of time management, delegating takes some up-front work, but if done correctly and in the right spirit, it has big payoffs.

Some people avoid delegating because they want something done in a certain way (their way) and because they want it done within a certain time frame (one under their control). But if you want members of your household to share in the responsibilities, you must loosen your grasp.

If anyone has ever delegated tasks to you, you probably know that there is a right way and a wrong way to delegate. No one wants high-priority tasks assigned at the last minute. No one wants to wait around to find out what's next on the list. Also, it's critical that the delegator understands—and is able to defend—his or her own use of time before asking for someone else's time. But if you've carried out the steps outlined in the section on time management, you qualify.

Ask Your Partner for Help

Women have been known to greet their partners at the door some evenings in tears of frustration. Men who took part in the survey said they don't know how to respond. If a man tries to help at that breaking point, it's too late, or the things he tries to do are insufficient, or he does them all wrong. So after exchanging words, the partners retreat to opposite ends of the house, angry and resentful. And the children suffer along with the romance.

A man will be much more inclined to help—and much more willing to learn how to help—if you go to him with solutions instead of with problems. Again, some up-front planning is needed.

As one man wrote: "Our relationship would be better if she would appreciate me and would not lay guilt trips on me or expect to have everything done her way."

The best time to decide that your partner needs to take a larger role in child-rearing and household duties is not when you are at your wit's end, but when you are calm, relaxed, and away from him and the children. Find some time alone, away from home. Get a baby-sitter, if you must, and take yourself to a coffee shop one afternoon with your quadrille pad and a pencil.

On a page of your pad, make three columns. In the first column, list every task that needs to be done on a regular basis for

the household, for the children, or for the relationship. Put in
as much detail as you can.
  Here's a sample list:

Grocery shopping
Meal preparation
Cleanup after meals
Keeping the home neat
Vacuuming
Dusting
Doing laundry
Mowing the lawn
Gardening
Attending PTA and other school functions
Attending parent/teacher meetings and following up on them
Chauffeuring (school, Scouts, sports, doctor appointments, etc.)
Helping the children with homework
Taking special time to teach the children
Caring for the children when they're sick
Clothes shopping for the children
Playing games or sports with the children
Reading to the children
Helping the children learn proper hygiene
Providing emotional support for the children
Spending time with families of the children's friends
Losing sleep (nighttime feedings, waiting up for teenagers, etc.)
Washing the car, filling the gas tank, auto maintenance
Paying the household bills
Providing financial support for the family
Keeping the social calendar
Making vacation plans
Maintaining household order

  Head the second column with your name and the third column with your partner's name. Now, going down the list of
tasks, fill in each blank column with a number that represents
the amount of time (in at least fifteen-minute chunks) that you

or your partner probably spends on each item on a weekly basis. Use the time record you developed earlier as a reference for your column. Estimate times for your partner.

Total each column to learn approximately how much time each of you spends on family and household. Remember, you are only estimating for your partner, and you may be off. But this isn't a list for him to see, so don't worry too much about that.

If your estimates tell you that your partner is contributing his fair share, make a point of congratulating him on it. Tell him about your discovery, and have a little reward ready for him tonight. Skip the rest of this section, and go directly to "Get Outside Help."

On the other hand, if you find that your partner could give you more support, read on.

Keep in mind that couples don't have to share family and household duties on a fifty-fifty basis. Assuming that the two of you live in the same household and the children are yours together, the goal is to share the big picture as equally as possible. Maybe you know that you're the best person to handle the emotional needs of the youngsters, but you feel that your partner could easily take over some of the grocery shopping or the chauffeuring or the playtime with the children. If one of you works longer hours outside the home than the other (this includes work-related projects done at home), that should be taken into consideration.

Now put a check mark next to times in your column when you would like your partner to help you. Also put a check mark next to times in his column when you would like to do more. The objective is a transfer of responsibility for certain areas; you aren't negotiating a one-shot vacuuming job.

Make a date with your partner to discuss household business at a place that's comfortable for both of you and where the children won't interrupt. If he probes for details about this upcoming rendezvous, let him know that you've become frustrated with your lack of time and that you've outlined an idea of how you can team up to expand your romance—for the sake of your relationship as well as for the sake of the family.

Presentation is important. Look your best. Wear something he likes to see you in. Better yet, wear something he gave you (jewelry, perfume, a blouse), and let him know how much you enjoy it. Focus on what you want to accomplish. Think of your partner as your audience. Make some mental notes ahead of time on how you might phrase your ideas. Present your situation as clearly and logically as you can. You might open with something like the following:

"We used to have so much fun together. Our relationship was filled with romance, and I miss that. But there's so little time and energy these days. I worry that I give everything to taking care of our home, raising the kids, and succeeding at my job, and I have nothing left for you."

How can he argue with that?

Continue along these lines: "I believe there may be some things we can do to create a happier situation. I'd like to hear your ideas on this, but the key issue for me is time. I just don't have as much time and energy to put into romance as I used to."

Here he may sympathize, agree, or even offer his help. If not, go on: "Sometimes I even feel resentful because I'm the one who spends so much time on the children and the housework. It may be my own doing: I'm so invested in it that I've probably shut you out. But lately I've been thinking about ways to bring back the old romance, and I'd like to get your feedback on a plan that I believe will help us."

You might ask him whether he is participating in household duties to the extent that he would like. If he says yes, then you've got a hard sell. Let him know how much you regret that you're neglecting him because of all you have to do for the children and household. (Keep *his* needs front and center.) If he asks how he might help out, suggest a few ways and gauge his response. Do *not* present him with a list that shows how little he is participating. If you must, refer to your notes about activities with which you can help each other.

If he doesn't want to add anything to his current responsibilities, you might ask him whether he will help you make a list that compares the time each of you spends on the children and house. If he agrees, write out all the family and household tasks again and let him fill in the times he thinks each of you spends. Then let him know how much time you actually spend on each item, based on keeping a detailed weeklong record.

If he is willing to take on new responsibilities but doesn't want to do the things that you earmarked for him, let him choose some others that will help you out. Give him options. Even if you don't come out of this process with a perfectly equal situation, you will have raised his level of consciousness. Furthermore, you will have a rational answer to his questions about whatever happened to that romance the two of you once had. He may not want to sign a contract with you on this, but he'll probably contribute more—on his own terms—than he did before the meeting.

As for any task that he agrees to do, let him know that you expect him to assume full responsibility for it. If he needs to know about deadlines or schedules (e.g., Jimmy has to be picked up from day care by 6:00 P.M.), make sure you write down the details.

A key to success: when your partner does decide to do more, let him do it his way. Unless he puts someone or something in danger, don't judge the way he chooses to contribute. If he's holding the baby on the right side instead of the left, or if he chooses the wrong kind of lettuce at the supermarket, don't criticize, or you'll lose all that you've gained. If the lettuce is really that important, go ahead and use the iceberg tonight, and next time make out a grocery list that specifies the exact type that you want. Be willing to take responsibility for letting him know what you need—but be flexible—and you'll have a happier man and a happier romance.

Another key: reward him for his efforts. For ideas, check out chapter 8, "Fifty Ways to Please Your Lover."

Get Outside Help

If your partner seems unwilling to or incapable of taking on more, or if what he offers isn't enough to free up your time, you have another option: Getting outside help. If your partner questions the need for this, review your discussion of frustration, romance, and the commitment to creating a happy home.

You might look into getting someone to watch the children. This can range from hiring a local high-school student on an hourly basis while you deal with housework or your own pursuits, to enrolling your child in day care either part- or full-time while you work. If you can afford it and you have the space, you might consider hiring a live-in helper (a student, a nanny, or an au pair) to care for the children and do some basic household chores.

Alternatively, you could find someone to come on a daily basis or once or twice a week to help you with the children or the household chores.

You can also get someone to come regularly to help keep your home clean. You can either hire a teenager to do some general housecleaning a few days a week after school while you take Junior for his afternoon walk or have a regular cleaning staff do a thorough job of dusting, vacuuming, window washing, oven cleaning, laundry, bathroom cleaning, floor washing, and whatever else you need done every few weeks.

You may be able to achieve some of the same benefits by trading services with your friends or neighbors. You're already quite aware, for example, of car pools. But what about trading cooking? You (and maybe your partner) could cook a neighbor's dinner and deliver it this Sunday evening, and then the neighbor could bring you dinner next Sunday evening. Other household chores can be arranged on the same basis. Take turns caring for each other's children—your turn this Saturday night, theirs the next. If you get along well with your neighbors, you can make all sorts of trades and arrangements: barter time walking the dogs, washing the cars, weeding the flower beds.

You could even combine services, so that each couple gets a real treat. You bring them dinner and take their kids this Saturday night; they bring you dinner and take your kids the following Saturday night. Now that's beginning to look a lot like romance.

One note of warning: Getting involved with others may create new time demands. It's imperative that you do not compromise your already hard-won daily schedule with new time-wasters. Don't add any tasks to your day unless the rewards are worth it.

Involve the Kids

Get your children involved in household responsibilities as soon as they are able. This is for their benefit as well as yours. In the beginning, it will take a lot longer for you to train and monitor your children than it would for you to accomplish the tasks on your own. Accept that. Bite your tongue when it takes them two hours to make their beds. Remember that both you and the children will be better in the end for the experience. The key for you is to know the children's capabilities and limitations, and you may want to consult their pediatrician to be sure.

Your children's first responsibilities may involve personal hygiene—brushing their own teeth, washing their own faces, and eventually bathing themselves. Along with this, you might teach them to wipe up the water splashed on the counter and mirror, to close the toothpaste cap, and to rinse and put away their toothbrushes. Teach them to leave a place as clean as they found it.

At the same time, they can learn how to keep their areas neat. They can put away their toys at the end of each play session, keep their clothes orderly in their closets and drawers, complete their homework, and keep their school supplies in the proper place. They can wipe their feet or take off their shoes when they enter the house, hang up their outdoor clothes, and put their dirty clothes into a hamper.

When they're a little older, they should be able to help with such household chores as setting the table, clearing dirty dishes from the dinner table, and feeding the dog. Soon they may be able to assist in preparing family meals, as well as sort their own laundry and fold their clean clothes.

This all involves time on your part, at least in the beginning, but the payoff is great for both you and your children. They'll learn respect for themselves and their surroundings, and you'll get a hand with the housework, which you can translate into time off.

A good model is the prototypical farm, where everyone has his or her own chores, and all must pull together in order for the farm to work. To the extent that you can, emulate that model in your own household, for it will not only provide you with a smoothly running operation, but it will also increase your children's respect for home as well as their self-esteem.

Activities to Hone Your Romantic Spirit

- Take stock of how you have asked your partner for help in the past. Learn from it.
- Make a list of all household and child-care tasks that need to be completed each week, and determine how much time you and your partner each spend on them. Determine where you need help, and for each of these tasks, decide whether he can provide the help or whether you need to hire someone.
- Make a date to meet your partner at a comfortable place where you will have time to discuss your concerns calmly.
- Investigate options for outside help.
- If you and your neighbors are friendly, see whether they would like to trade child care or meal preparation. (Or approach your friends about this.) However, be sure that such an arrangement wouldn't compromise your new commitment to time management.
- As soon as your children are capable, involve them in household chores. Make a list for them to check off as they accomplish each daily task. Train them to do things properly, and follow through with rewards, such as coupons for their favorite foods, games, and stories, or letting them stay up half an hour past bedtime to play.

- Make a book of coupons for favors your partner would like from you, and give him one each time he is of special help to you.

Setting Personal Goals

Now that you've eliminated your time-wasters, prioritized your tasks, and delegated responsibility, what are you going to do with all that bonus time?

As your children grow older, take more responsibility for themselves, and eventually leave the nest, what do you intend to do with the rest of your life? Setting goals is the first step to ensuring that when the time comes, you've got a life.

If you think that this will interfere with your relationship, it may surprise you to learn that more than 80 percent of the men surveyed said that it is important to their relationship for their partner to "pursue her own interests" and "show independence." Percentages were highest for married men, whether or not there were children living at home.

So get that quadrille pad out again. On a clean sheet, write down everything of importance that you ever wanted to do or be. Include all the interests and activities that have shaped your life. Add to these items all the things that you still dream of creating or becoming. Your personal goals will probably fall into the following categories:

- Family: goals for your children as well as a good, strong, lasting romance;
- Education: skills or degrees that could help you attain intellectual or career goals;
- Career: positions you might want to attain in a company, or entrepreneurial activities you may want to pursue;
- Health of body and spirit: ways to improve the well-being of your family as well as health goals for yourself;
- Friendships: keeping up with long-term friendships and building new ones;

- Leisure: making time for your favorite activities and learning new ones;
- Society: volunteer work to help better the lives of others or to improve and protect the environment.

Don't worry about being silly or wanting too much. Envision everything you could possibly desire from life. Because if you can't envision something, you will never achieve it.

When you're finished writing, you may have a terribly long list that looks impossible to get through. Take heart. Time management allows you to break these large goals into increments that you can accomplish on a weekly or even a daily basis. The key is to keep your goals in sight and to keep working toward them.

To take one goal as a general example, look at health. This category may include lots of changes for your whole family, but focus on yourself right now. You may want to get in better shape. If so, your goal will probably involve changes in your eating habits (which may or may not take up time) as well as a stepped-up exercise routine (which will definitely demand time).

When setting your daily or weekly goals, be specific. Instead of writing, "I want to lose weight," write "I will weigh 120 pounds by September." Be realistic, however, or you'll set yourself up for failure. Also, make sure that you can accomplish your incremental goals without impairing your health or interfering with your other priorities.

The incremental steps for your health goal may look something like this:

- Week one: Talk to your physician about your ideal weight and your capacity for a shape-up program.
- Week two: Check out your exercise options. Is there a good aerobics show on TV at a time that's convenient for you (or can you record it to watch later)? Is there a good audiocassette or videotape you could purchase? Can you

buy a few light weights and a book on weight training? Can you afford the money and space for weight training equipment and, if so, would you use it? If you joined a local gym, would you go regularly? (Some gyms offer child care, but is it good care?) Does your bicycle need a tune-up? Do you need a new pair of walking shoes, hiking boots, or cross-country skis?

- Week three: Make some decisions, and discuss arrangements with your partner. (Do you need him to watch the children while you're exercising? Would he join you in a family membership at the gym?) Make necessary purchases. Put exercise activities on your calendar (for example, three days of aerobics class, two working out with weights, Sunday bike ride with the family).
- Week four: Maintain exercise schedule. Take a look at your eating habits. Note the fat content of the foods you eat (read labels).
- Week five: Maintain exercise schedule. Go to your local bookstore to investigate lowfat cookbooks and magazines on healthy eating. Pick up a guide on fat and calories. Make yourself some lowfat snacks to munch during the day. Begin to plan some lowfat menus.
- Week six: Maintain exercise schedule. Make at least one lowfat meal for yourself.
- Week seven: Maintain exercise schedule. Make at least one lowfat dinner for your family.
- Week eight: Maintain exercise schedule. Make at least two lowfat meals for your family. Encourage your partner to initiate healthful eating habits.

Now you've been at this for two months. You're on your way to looking good, and you're enjoying the way you feel, as well.

During this process, you should gradually integrate other life goals into your daily schedule. Maybe you've investigated painting courses (you always wanted to be an artist). Or you and your partner have started taking a dance class (that counts for exercise *and* romance). Maybe you're helping with your daughter's school play, you spend an hour a week as a teacher's aide, or you volunteer at the school library.

You look better, your self-esteem is soaring, and you have energy to romance that guy you love. That's how it works. You're doing more than you ever thought you could, yet you have time for romance, too.

Activities to Hone Your Romantic Spirit

- List your personal goals for the coming year.
- Break down each of your goals into small—and then smaller—steps that you can handle on a daily basis. Accomplishing each step shouldn't take more than an hour or two.
- Start a weekly program that will move you toward your goals. Put at least one small step from each goal on each weekly list. Check off incremental goals as you realize them.
- After a few weeks, evaluate your progress. If you aren't accomplishing your incremental goals, try to determine why. If it's because you're asking too much of yourself, assign yourself smaller increments or limit the number of goals you can work toward at one time. If you are procrastinating, ask yourself whether this goal is really as important as you thought. What are the benefits of doing what you've failed to do? If they're insufficient, you may want to reassess this goal. But if you have kept up with your plan, reward yourself.
- Share your plans with your partner. Let him know how working toward your personal goals will enliven your romance with him. And tell him how much you appreciate his support.
- Make arrangements to spend evenings alone with your partner on a regular basis.
- Arrange with your family for a regular time—as little as fifteen minutes a day—that you can spend by yourself,

without anyone calling for help. Let everyone know that this is *your* time. If you spend it at home, you may want to unplug your phone and put a "Do Not Disturb" sign on your door. If someone else is available to mind the children, you may choose to walk, bike, or drive to a solitary spot where you can gain some inner peace.

7

Practicing Romance Every Day

Romance isn't something that happens only once in a while, when everything is working right. In fact, it doesn't happen at all unless someone makes it happen. It might even take some planning at first, and it might take a little time. But once you have the spirit, it will come easily.

Romance is an attitude that you can create anywhere, anytime. If you start it, your partner is sure to follow. One small romantic act can serve as a catalyst, and soon your relationship will resonate with an electrifying glow.

The trick is to make it a habit. As revealed in the first two chapters, men need tender loving care and attention. Giving your partner a little TLC every day shows that you truly care for him. In time this will strengthen your relationship, expanding its romantic power.

One of the men who responded to the survey summarized the need to strive for daily romance this way:

Day-to-day life—with careers, children, chores, bills, and all those horribly mundane things that stress and strain—means that a couple has to make a conscious commitment to make romance a part of their lives. My romantic fantasy is not some special place or occasion, such as a remote beach in Hawaii, but to have romance continue as an integral part of our lives, so that time is set aside each day to care for each other. No matter how simple or elaborate, it's not so much the setting but the feeling and attention, where we affirm daily, "You are important to me, I enjoy having you in my life, and I want to take time to celebrate our relationship even if only for a short while each day." It means never taking each other for granted, and it means always caring for and nurturing each other and being supportive of each other. It's keeping romance alive in our daily living that matters the most. It's all the little things that constantly remind us that we matter to each other.

Lasting romance exists in a continuum of small, loving actions carried out on a regular basis. Opportunities to spontaneously romance your partner are all around you. Something as seemingly inconsequential as using his name in conversation can add intimacy to your relationship. Giving him a special greeting, without complaining about your problems, can trigger romantic feelings.

This chapter brings together some of the most important aspects of romance that you can practice on a daily basis. Move toward your partner in romance, and then move away in order to give him enough room to romance you in return. In this way you create an easy-flowing reciprocal interplay that will develop the intimacy of your relationship.

If, on a *daily* basis, you make him feel better with you than he feels when he is with anyone else, where do you think he'll want to spend his time and attention?

Being There

If you think you have to leave the house to be romantic, you're missing the greatest opportunities for enhancing your love relationship. If romance can happen spontaneously at home, you've got a lot of romance coming.

Greet Him

Whenever you've been away from your partner for even an hour, greet him as you come together again. When he walks through the door, go to him, give him a hug and a kiss, look into his eyes, say his name. If he's been away for more than a day, tell him that you missed him. If you're the one arriving home, go find him and give him a proper greeting.

Look happy when you greet him. Let your facial expressions and gestures show that you're glad to see him, that you appreciate your relationship with him, that you enjoy his company. Of the men surveyed, 87 percent said that it was important for their partner to hug them. And, as mentioned in chapter 5, more than 90 percent of the men surveyed said it was important that their partner "be fun to be around." Percentages were highest for men with children living at home.

If you and your partner aren't in the habit of greeting each other, start by going to him and saying hello or giving him a little kiss. If you keep this up, the rest will follow. Acknowledge him when you first see one another after work each evening, when you meet for a date, or when either of you has been away on a trip. Make meeting an important occasion. And as the days and weeks go by, you'll find that the rewards of greeting him will go a long way toward increasing the romantic element of your relationship.

The everyday greeting is key. But if he's been gone longer than a few days, you have a great opportunity to show him how much you appreciate him. In answering the question "Has there ever been a time when your partner made you feel particularly special?" survey respondents produced examples of this:

> "She gave me the most wonderful Welcome Home card with a love poem she had written."

> "She had banners all over the front hallway and a big Welcome Home sign. It may sound a little silly, but knowing that she went to that trouble to let me know that she was glad to have me back really felt good."

> "She picked me up at the airport and brought me home to a terrific dinner she had prepared for me."

Make Him Your Hero

Once in a while your partner may have a story to tell about a special achievement: he finished the report, made a breakthrough, won the case. On these occasions, let him tell it without interruption. Listen to everything he has to say. Give him a hug for all the barriers he had to overcome in order to reach his goal. Tell him you're proud of him.

But most days are probably pretty mundane for him. There's nothing important to report, he didn't accomplish anything of note, and he doesn't feel like the hero he wants to be. Hence he may become annoyed if you pepper him with questions about his day. He may become downright angry if you suggest that he could have done something this way rather than that way.

Instead of offering opinions that he didn't request, let him know in small ways, every day, that you respect his capabilities and appreciate his contributions. Let him know that he is your hero.

One survey respondent put this at the top of the list of things his partner does to make him feel special: "She has a good opinion about me, and she lets everyone know every chance she gets. I've even overheard her telling her friends how great I am, and it really does make me feel special."

From another: "My girlfriend sometimes will make a comment about me out of the blue. She'll look up from whatever she's doing and say, 'You're absolutely beautiful!' or 'It feels so good just being here with you.' These times mean more to me than anything else."

If you make him feel good when he's with you, he will want to be with you more often.

Support Him in Defeat

There will be days when your partner comes home from work with his tail between his legs. You might ask whether anything is wrong. If you have demonstrated to him in the past that he can trust you—you restrained yourself from questioning his methods or attempting to solve his problems—he may be open to sharing his concerns with you.

If he doesn't want to talk about it, let it go. But be sure to let him know that if he does decide to talk about it at some point, you would like to listen. Give him a rain check that means you will be available for him anytime. If and when he opens up, show him that you are his ally, not his foe.

Be his cheerleader, even if he does occasionally drop the ball. Remind him of his good points, and build him up. Help him feel strong and successful.

One survey respondent wrote: "There are two times I recall that my partner made me feel particularly special. The first occurred at a time when I was going through a lousy period at work. She left a voice-mail message for me to find in the middle of a terrible day, letting me know that she was thinking about me and that she cared. The other was the first time she told me that she loved me."

Keep Current on His Activities

Keep current on his job and outside interests so that you will be more interested in hearing about them. This doesn't mean pummeling him with questions every time you see him. It means paying attention to what he says when he voluntarily talks about his day. If his job or favorite activity entails something unfamiliar to you, you might want to read up on it. Learn about the role his type of work or his avocation plays in the general scheme of things so that you can better understand him.

But, whatever you do, if it's his line of work (or play) and not yours, let him be the one who knows best. If you are truly interested and have questions, by all means ask. He'll probably enjoy being the teacher. And if you have children old enough to understand, try to get them interested in what he does. It will add greatly to the dinnertime conversation, and it might start the youngsters thinking about their own future work. Best of all, it will help them respect and appreciate their dad as fully as you do.

Appreciate the Little Things

Whenever your partner does something special for you, for your home, or for the family, let him know how much you appreciate it. Remember, for a man, doing favors and chores is an expression of love. Instead of *saying* the "I love you," he *does* it. A few examples from survey respondents illustrate this:

> "I don't mind doing things around the house because my partner always gives me lots of credit for it."

> "I help her whenever I can, and she always makes me feel that it was time well spent."

> "After I spent a lot of time sponge-painting the living room, my partner had a party and invited all the neighbors to show them what a great job I had done. Now I'm planning to paint the master bedroom. She's out choosing the colors right now."

> "Whenever I'm around when she uses the garbage disposal, she reminds me how important it is to her and how terrific it was that I fixed it."

> "We take turns making dinner and cleaning up. Every time, even if I haven't put a big effort into the cooking, she tells me how much she appreciates the time I spend to please her. And when I make something she really likes, I hear about that real fast. So I don't mind doing my share."

Give him kudos for washing your car today, and a few days later follow it up with, "It's so nice to have a clean car again." He'll know you really mean it.

Congratulate him for teaching the children a new skill, even if it's only how to play a new board game. Praise him for helping the children with their homework, and sometime later tell him that you respect his efforts to help them achieve goals. When they earn good grades, remind him of his role in teaching them.

In addition, if he helps you with your own work, let him know that you respect his ideas and appreciate his assistance.

Knowing that actions speak louder than words for men, you might want to say, "I feel your love when you do that for me," anytime your partner helps you out. You will find that the more you show appreciation for his help, the more he will want to help.

Activities to Hone Your Romantic Spirit

- Start paying attention to greetings. If you and your partner don't already greet each other lovingly when you come together, start small. Eventually he'll respond in kind, and exchanging an affectionate greeting will become a habit.

- At the end of the day, let him know that he is your hero whether or not he accomplished anything special. Let him know that you appreciate his capabilities, his goals, and his causes.
- When he has problems at work, listen without judging. Don't try to solve everything. This is the best possible time to show him that your love is unconditional.
- Keep current on his line of work, so that you can better understand him when he opens up to you about it.

Giving Him Special Treatment

Show your partner how much he matters to you by giving him special time and attention at home. This will not only enhance romance, but it will also help him feel safe enough to develop true intimacy with you.

Set Aside Time for Him

You have so much to do and so little time. But it's critical that you set aside some time for your partner every day that you're together. This is time for the two of you just to relax, with no agenda.

One survey respondent summed up what many had to say about romance: "The romantic times I appreciate most involve staying home together with my wife, having a quiet candlelit dinner, and then sipping wine by the fire."

This isn't a time for you to talk about your problems and concerns. This is time that you are giving to your partner. Sit quietly next to him, and just be together. Even fifteen minutes of shared quiet time every day will go a long way toward letting him know that you appreciate his company.

There are also times when he wants to be alone. He may best unwind from a difficult day by working in the garage or sitting in front of his computer screen. So if he brushes you off, don't despair. Plan a quiet time for later, after he comes out of his "cave."

In order to make room for this precious time, take a look at your schedule and get rid of low-priority activities and time-wasters. Organize your work spaces. Order projects and errands so that you can do them in batches. Find ways to manage your work more efficiently, and you'll have more time for romance.

Touch Him with Tenderness

Because men don't readily express their emotions, they often carry them in their bodies. And because they have learned to suppress their feelings, they may not even realize how tight their shoulders, backs, and feet become during the day.

Your partner would probably be thrilled to come home to a shoulder rub, a foot rub, or a massage. Massage is wonderful not only because it relieves your partner's sore muscles and stress from daily cares, but also because it provides an opportunity for him to be in close physical contact with you without the pressure to have sex. In fact, more than 75 percent of men surveyed said that it was important for their partner to "touch me in nonsexual ways."

One man wrote, "Usually when I have had a very stressful day at work, my wife will give me a massage, and it helps me relax and enjoy the evening with the family."

This is a great way to enhance the intimacy of your relationship. And if he wants to reciprocate, that's nice, too. In fact, responding to the question "What could you tell your partner that would improve your relationship?" more than a few men wrote, "Let's touch more!"

Invite Him Home

Whether or not you live together, write up an invitation for a great at-home date and send it to your partner by U.S. mail or by e-mail, or leave it among his things where he's sure to find it. Do this at least a few days in advance.

Make arrangements so that you can be together alone. Make sure the baby is sound asleep and all other members of the household are elsewhere.

Take time to relax and prepare before your partner shows up. (If he rarely leaves home, send him on an errand—maybe to pick up a special bottle of wine or a great dessert.)

Wear something special. Put on a spritz of perfume. Add something he gave you—a piece of jewelry, perhaps.

Take the initiative in meal-planning. Cook something special, pick up something already prepared, or have something delivered. If you two enjoy preparing meals together, plan for that, add a little flirting, and you're on your way.

Throughout the meal—throughout the entire evening, for that matter—focus on your partner. Avoid discussions of problems, concerns, or differences.

Feed him from your fork. Touch him under the table. Flirt.

You might plan an after-dinner activity, such as a board game you both enjoy, a walk in the moonlight, or special music in front of the fire. But just giving him your complete attention will make him happy indeed.

Value His Gifts to You

If he has given you jewelry, perfume, or clothing, take good care of these things and wear them often. When you have them on, make a special effort to let him know how much you value them. "I love how this dress brings out my eyes," you might say, or "Look how terrific these earrings are," followed by a wink.

From one survey respondent: "On our fifth wedding anniversary, I gave my wife a gold bracelet. She put it on that night and hasn't taken it off in the three years since. She wears it every day. It's obvious to me that she appreciates the gift, but it's more than that. For me, it's a symbol—like our wedding rings—of her care for me."

Your partner wants to know that he gives you pleasure. There have doubtless been many times in his life when he has missed the mark, especially when it comes to choosing gifts.

But you can help him figure out what you want, and you can show your appreciation for his attempts to satisfy your desires.

Don't blame him if he isn't catching your hints. When there's something you really want or need, let him know in a way that's sure to carry the message. If he doesn't respond to "Oh, isn't that pretty," or "I could use one of those," then try saying, "I'd love it if you gave me something like that sometime," or "It would be great if you did that for me." Most men will appreciate the directness, since it helps them please you.

Develop Common Interests

If, aside from home and children, you and your partner don't share any interests on a regular basis, you might want to look into finding a sport or activity that you both would enjoy.

You could take a class together to learn something new, or you could join a team or club to revive a skill from the past. Ballroom dancing, softball, scuba diving, tennis, crossword puzzles, bridge, bicycling: there are so many options that you're sure to find something to please both of you. A morning run or an evening walk will do, so long as you make it a habit.

One survey respondent wrote about the dominoes game that he and his partner take with them whenever they travel. Playing dominoes has become their way to relax together without having to plan anything. Such a game can travel as easily to a posh resort as to a mountain peak.

Be on Time

Emotion came through in the survey when men rated the importance of being on time. Of course, not all women are chronically late, and you may be the punctual exception, but the word is out that women in general just don't know how to handle time.

"Most women I've dealt with in relationships don't have any sense of time. They don't know how to measure it or plan for it," wrote one man. "And women say that men can't commit . . . ," wrote another.

About 60 percent of men surveyed rated it important that their partner "be on time," and many of those who did added exclamation points and other indications of strong feelings.

What bothers a man about tardiness is the implication that his time isn't as important as your time. In fact, he often perceives it as a real discount of himself. For some, this brings a sense that being with him is not important to you. Arriving fashionably late might be appropriate for social gatherings, but it's not appropriate treatment for your partner.

If you find that you are chronically late, you may need to evaluate your sense of time and upgrade your planning skills. Unless you are subconsciously doing this on purpose (and you'll need a therapist to help you out there), just changing your attitude can do wonders. Start thinking of yourself as the on-time one rather than the late one. Follow through and make it happen.

This is one change your partner is sure to appreciate.

Activities to Hone Your Romantic Spirit

- Each evening, when your partner signals that he has spent enough time alone to rid himself of his daily cares, go sit beside him for about fifteen minutes, just being with him. Discard any expectations. Smile. Then, before you leave him to go back to whatever you had been doing, give him a little kiss.
- Learn a few new recipes that call for some of your partner's favorite foods, and surprise him when he least expects it.
- Touch him with tenderness: greet him after work with a massage, a shoulder rub, or a foot rub. Let his cares melt away in your hands.
- Flirt. And if you're already flirting with each other, flirt more. Show him how much fun you have being with him.
- At least once a week, plan a special date night at home.
- If you are in the habit of wearing sloppy clothes and not attending to your looks when you spend evenings with

your partner, make a special effort to enhance your appearance for him at least once a week.

- When your partner pleases you with a gift, use it often. Each time you do, remind him again of your appreciation.
- If you have difficulty keeping time commitments, try to determine why that is and begin to plan for change.

Staying in the Present

So much of our time and energy is taken up with regretting the past or planning for the future. Too often, we let little chances for romance pass us by. You can remedy this situation by taking advantage of the present.

Make Romance a Daily Priority

True romance is possible only if it is an integral part of your relationship. It doesn't happen at the snap of a finger. It can't wait for the Caribbean cruise. Rather, it is a steady, practiced way of life. From the moment you greet each other upon waking until you kiss each other goodnight, this way of living requires a romantic attitude, a romantic spirit throughout the day.

Unfortunately, romance is often swept under the rug by the innumerable time-consuming demands that appear to be greater priorities. Know that your partner wants to be your priority. Every moment that you are with him, you are either working toward a better romance or you are working against it.

Romancing is usually left up to the man. But according to survey respondents, men would like it otherwise. As one wrote, "I wish she would take some initiative in the role of the romancer. I personally enjoy romancing her, but I'd like to be romanced once in a while, too."

In today's hectic world, you must make a daily commitment to maintaining romance.

Enjoy the Moment

Spend an entire day in the present. If you say something, be aware that you're speaking in the present tense, with no regrets for what has happened or plans for the future. If your partner or your children speak of past or future, let it go. You don't have to tell them what you're up to, but you can try to bring them into the present as well.

Enjoy your time with your family. Listen to what they say without thinking of how you will respond. Teach your children without the threat of punishment.

Enjoy your dinner without worrying about who will do the dishes or what you will do later in the evening.

Enjoy any little touches or acts of love as they occur without wondering what they mean. Give love without expecting anything in return.

The present is a good place to be. Don't lose it, or you may live your future regretting the past.

Don't Wait for an Occasion

Give your partner a special gift today, for no reason. Here are a few suggestions:

- A little kiss when he least expects it;
- One of his chores—completed by you;
- His favorite snack or dessert;
- Tickets for the two of you to attend one of his favorite events;
- A poem or love note that you composed.

A thoughtful surprise reminds him that you care.

Tell Him You Care

Call him up and tell him you love him. Do it in the middle of the day, without expecting anything in return. About 70 percent of survey respondents said it was important that their partner "keeps in touch when we are apart."

Don't talk about your day, your problems, or your plans. Just say, "I've been thinking about you, and I just wanted you to know that I love you." After he responds, let him know that you're looking forward to seeing him tonight or this weekend or whenever you will be with him next.

Then, when you are with him, tell him about some of his traits that you particularly admire. You may never have vocalized your admiration for many of his most endearing characteristics, such as:

- Physical attributes: eyes (color, depth, twinkle), hair (texture, thickness, color), hands (shape, capabilities), body (strength, physique), skin (color, feel), athletic skills, health, energy;
- Emotional capabilities: to experience joy, to express emotions, to control anger, to forgive, to demonstrate power, to understand, to be adventurous, to be patient, to love;
- Social capabilities: friendliness, manners, charm, conversational style, wit, ability to articulate ideas, thoughtfulness, generosity, honesty, tact, responsibility, leadership, diplomacy, respect, playfulness, open-mindedness, adaptability;
- Mental capabilities: knowledge, problem-solving, patience, creativity, brightness, sense of wonder, ingenuity, inventiveness, imagination, boldness, self-reliance, objectivity, efficiency, resourcefulness, reason, understanding, ability to remain coolheaded, self-awareness, reliance, confidence, determination;
- Spiritual capabilities: generosity, maturity, self-awareness, helpfulness, idealism, honorableness, piety, fidelity, modesty, optimism, charity, inner strength, forgiveness, ability to love.

These are only some examples of the traits that your own partner may exhibit. Which of his traits do you value most? Which are most important to him?

Praise his attributes. Celebrate his accomplishments. Acknowledge his talents. Recognize his uniqueness. Show him the beautiful truths about himself that maybe he hasn't even realized.

According to Dr. Daphne Rose Kingma, "The praise you need to give isn't just the obvious praise, that he's handsome or smart, that he always pays the bills on time. The praise that will free a man and heal him, that will open him up to his feelings and make him feel safe enough to open his heart in your presence, is praise for the things he's never been acknowledged for, the attributes that are still invisible to him, the beautiful truths in himself he's forgotten or never quite remembered."

Compliment him whenever you are reminded of his fine traits. Whisper your admiration in the dark between the sheets. Write your appreciation into love notes, and leave them for him to find. Tell him: "When you held me last night, I was swept away by your strength"; "I was touched just watching you help Mrs. Johnson across the street"; "I hope you know that Bobby thinks you're the smartest dad in the world . . . and so do I!"

This is intimacy his way. And he'll love you for it.

Let Your Self-Confidence Shine Through

Again and again, men have said that they enjoy being with a woman who is comfortable with herself, confident of her views, and not afraid to say no. But all too often, women are reticent about approaching their partner romantically because they are focusing on their own flaws: "I can't romance him today because I'm not perfect yet." They fear looking foolish, being rejected, feeling silly.

Your partner was drawn to you because of your attractiveness—mental, emotional, physical, spiritual. Most likely it was a combination of your many unique personal qualities that brought him to your side. And even if your courtship was years ago, that core attractiveness is still there for him, if only you would let it shine through. Remember that it's much easier to love someone who loves herself.

In response to the open-ended survey question "What could you tell your partner that would improve your relationship?" quite a few men spoke of this very concern.

One man wrote, "Do relax around me—I'm fun and I'm not hung up on how you look or what your job is. I'm interested in you. Looking good and being attractive is a wonderful bonus, but it's only a bonus, not an ante. Besides, I don't want to feel obliged to keep up with/match you in an effort to look good or to act perfectly."

Instead of appreciating their own attributes, women frequently call attention to what they perceive as their flaws. When a woman does that, her partner may eventually come to agree with her estimation of herself.

If you can and want to change some of your traits or qualities, then, by all means, set the appropriate goals and pursue them step-by-step. But as to the characteristics that you cannot change, or don't truly want to change, accept them and move on.

If you focus on your positive traits, you will feel more confident in yourself, you will be more attractive to your partner, and you will be much more inclined to initiate romance with him.

If you take responsibility for your own happiness, you have a great chance of being happy.

Thank Him for Compliments

When your partner says, "Hey, that dress looks great on you," he doesn't want to hear, "What, this old rag?" And when he compliments you on an accomplishment, don't respond with, "You don't know the half of it," or, "Yeah, and where were you when I was working so hard?" Such responses will only diminish what he is telling you and close him down—maybe forever.

Start accepting his compliments. Instead of beginning with, "Yes, but . . ." (which is actually a correction of his lack of judgment), enhance your relationship with, "I'm glad you like the way I look," or something similar that will tell him you not only appreciate his compliment but you also trust his judgment. His compliment is a gift. Accept it openly, with a positive statement.

If he doesn't give you as many compliments as you'd like, think about the ways you have responded in the past. Some alternative responses might be: "I appreciate that," "I can always count on you to perk me up," or simply, "Thank you."

Take Advantage of Nature

Nearly everything about nature is romantic—the sweet chirps of a bird, the wild sound of a storm, the view of a mountain, the dark silence of a woods, ripples on a body of water. Snow, rain, wind. Moonlight, starlight, sunlight. Sharing the elements can add intimacy to your romance.

Nature is all around you. You need not go far. You need only take notice.

If you don't already enjoy the outdoors together, start walking early in the morning or before or after dinner in the evening. If walking isn't your speed, try jogging around the neighborhood, bicycling across town, or hiking through a park.

If you have children, get them involved. Take the baby in the stroller, on the bike seat behind yours, or in the baby carrier. Let the older youngsters ride their bikes while you walk or jog alongside. If you've got a sleeping baby in the next room, you might not want to venture beyond the back porch, but you can still watch the stars or catch a few snowflakes.

Enjoying nature together is a good way to stay connected. So start now. After dinner tonight, invite your partner to take a walk with you in the moonlight or the snow or the rain. Don't talk about anything unless he starts the conversation. Let the night air work the romance. At the top of the hill (or in the park or in front of the best view), take his hand. Look up at him and smile. Breathe in the romance.

Try Taking the Lead

Initiate lovemaking.

Don't wait until you're both in bed and he's ready to go to sleep. Start flirting right now. Put on some alluring clothes. Smile as if you have a secret. And don't stop when you get to bed. Let him know that you mean business.

This may be a new beginning for both of you.

End with a Kiss

If you don't already exchange a good-night kiss every night you're together, start now. This simple act cuts right through all the daily aggravations and says, "I'm glad to be here with you." It's a great habit.

By the way, in spite of the fact that many men are less than expressive about their own feelings, nearly 90 percent of survey respondents said it was important that their partner "tell me she loves me."

Activities to Hone Your Romantic Spirit

- Spend a day focusing on the present. Be aware of the sights, the sounds, and the smells all around you, and the way your body feels. Practice living in the present with your partner. Focus on now.
- Create a little gift—something simple—that will make him smile. Give it to him today.
- The next time you speak with your partner, whether in person or on the phone, tell him that you love him. Let him know that you're glad he is in your life today.
- Practice saying "Thank you."
- Praise your partner for something, however small, every day.
- Find a time to ask him to go outside with you—to smell the roses, to look at the stars, or to hike to the hilltop.

- Review chapter 4, "Fueling the Flame," and initiate sex when you're together tonight.
- Take stock of yourself. Make a list of your characteristics that bother you at times. Note which of them you can and are willing to change and which of them you will simply have to accept as part of your uniqueness. Begin a plan both to change what you can and accept what you either can't or don't want to change. Then make a list of all your positive traits—physical, intellectual, creative, spiritual, special capabilities, skills, and so on. Whenever you are feeling less than wonderful, focus on these to boost your spirits. And the next time you feel like complaining about one of your flaws—to yourself or to your partner—mention one of your positive traits instead.
- Start a good-night kiss ritual. Even if you've been arguing, even if his back is turned to you, even if he doesn't respond for days, just do it.

8

Fifty Ways to Please Your Lover

Men are delighted by unexpected romance and passion. The spontaneous act that says, "I'm thinking about you right now," evokes a man's appreciation for the joy his partner brings.

There are certainly lots of ways you can please your partner, and from the many ways listed in this chapter, you should be able to find at least fifty little things that you can do right now to let your partner know that you mean romance. In spite of the short time it takes to implement any one of these ideas, each can make a big impact, as well as a lasting impression.

Some of them involve a little risk, so start with the ones with which you feel most comfortable: you need to know your own capabilities as well as what your partner would appreciate. Don't think you have to try them all; choose among those that will be fun for both you and your partner.

As your romantic spirit grows, you're sure to start thinking up your own quick tricks for romancing that great guy. And you may just find him giving a little more thought to romancing *you*.

- Once a day this week, touch him when he least expects it. Today maybe you'll run your fingers through his hair, tomorrow caress his face, the next day touch his arm while he's speaking. Get into it. Watch his response.
- Call him at work just to say hello.

- Sit next to him in silence. Read, knit, do a crossword puzzle, or work on your latest project, while you let him quietly enjoy your company.
- Create an atmosphere for love tonight.
- The next time you're away from him for more than a few days, send him a love letter that tells him how important he is to your happiness.
- If you have children living at home, plan some special time to spend as a family.
- Pick up some little thing for his favorite sport or hobby, and put it where he'll find it when he goes out to play.
- When he does something you appreciate, tell him. Thank him. Let him know that you're glad he was there to help.
- Put on something sexy tonight just for him.
- The next time you make love, tell him what you enjoy most about his lovemaking.
- Invite him for a walk. Enjoy the sunrise, sunshine, moonlight, starlight, rain, snow, or wind together.
- Stay in bed a little longer than usual on a weekend morning to talk about your dreams—and listen to his.
- Play his favorite music during dinner.
- Cuddle with no expectations.
- Initiate a day trip away from your usual environment. Explore together. Focus on the present.
- Be in a happy, outgoing mood when he arrives home.
- Invite him on a date to his favorite restaurant or one that he wants to try. Over dinner, discuss only subjects that interest him.
- Plan an evening home alone together, and rent a film that will stimulate his senses.
- Wear something he gave you (e.g., jewelry, clothing, perfume), and let him know how much you enjoy it.
- Invite him to dance with you in the living room—or on the back porch in the moonlight.
- While you're out shopping, pick up something that will make him smile. Present it to him the next time you're alone together.

- Does he like to wake up to a cup of coffee or tea, or a glass of orange juice? Tomorrow morning, before he goes to make it himself, prepare it and bring it to him.
- If you want sex with him now (or a little later), go for it. Make the moves that will show him what you want. Set the atmosphere. Get rid of distractions. Call ahead with a sexy message. Wear something alluring. Flirt. Whisper sweet nothings into his ear. Touch him.
- Invite him to help you plan a terrific outing or vacation for just the two of you.
- Do something for him that he usually does for himself. Get the car washed, mow the lawn, take out the garbage—any chore you feel comfortable doing.
- Ask him to help you with something that takes physical strength or brainpower, a task that will enhance his masculine pride. It may involve lifting, carrying, planning, solving, or repairing. Then show your appreciation for his help.
- Have his favorite photo of you framed (or have one taken and framed), and leave it near the things he takes to work.
- Spend an evening focusing on him. Don't mention any of your own problems or concerns. Let him talk. And if he doesn't start, ask him questions that will bring out his goals, desires, and concerns.
- Obtain two tickets (good seats) to one of his favorite athletic or cultural events. Send them to him in a handmade invitation to have you as his escort.
- Polish his shoes (or stick a coupon that says, "good for one polishing," into a pair of shoes that needs it).
- When he comes home tonight, tell him to relax. You'll take care of everything.
- On the way to a party or a restaurant or the movies, let him know that you're not wearing underwear.
- Learn how to cut his hair—the way he wants it cut.
- Get yourself a black brassiere, a black garter belt, black stockings, black high heels, and a little white apron.

Wear only these while cooking and serving a special dinner for him.

- Iron his shirts.
- Give him a compliment he hasn't heard before.
- Invite him to play a game of strip poker.
- When you greet each other in the evening, refrain from telling him about your day before he tells you about his.
- Invite him to a night at the drive-in. Wear something sexy.
- Open a savings account for that big vacation you always wanted.
- The next time you will be away from him during a meal, make him something special and leave it in the refrigerator for him to find.
- Get home before he does today, and make a special effort to look fresh and attractive for him.
- Wash his car.
- Touch him in a nonsexual way.
- Take him clothes shopping, and let him choose something for you to buy for him.
- Ask him to explain one of his hobbies or interests to you.
- Act playful.
- Massage his feet.
- When he's feeling low, tell him about something that's wonderful about him.
- Invite him on a picnic.
- Give him a book of coupons for "services" you are willing to provide whenever he desires to redeem a coupon. (Be specific about the services!)
- Let him choose the movie this weekend.
- Leave a very sexy message on his private answering machine, telling him exactly what you want to do with him. Be prepared to follow through!
- Let him sleep late on Saturday morning while you keep the house quiet, and then invite him to enjoy the terrific brunch you prepared.
- Write a poem for him, and hide it in his briefcase, under his dinner plate, on his dashboard, in the book he's reading, or under the covers on his side of the bed.

- Run a bath for him, and wash his hair.
- Think up something special to do that shows him how fun you are to be around.
- Buy a small, pretty oil-burning lamp and the appropriate oil, place it on your nightstand, light the wick before he comes to bed, and turn out the light.
- The next time you and your partner are out with a group, mention something wonderful about him to someone else, making sure that your partner hears you.
- Call him in the middle of the day from a motel, and let him know that you'll be waiting for him whenever he gets off work.
- Bring home a bottle of his favorite wine or other drink to have with dinner.
- Wake him a little earlier than usual one morning by snuggling up to him.
- Read to him from a book of erotic poems or stories.
- Prepare his favorite meal for him—in style.
- Give him a good, long massage. Try using scented massage oil and lighting scented candles.
- Before he arrives home, leave a trail of your clothes from the front door to wherever he'll find you.
- Give him a special, quiet time-out. Leave the house (take the children with you), and tell him to relax and do whatever he wants to do.
- Make plans with him for a great escape—just the two of you—even if it's only a weekend away from home.
- The next time you spend a day together, spend it secretly thinking of all his wonderful qualities and capabilities, and smile every time he looks your way.
- Put a candle on the dinner table.
- Find a portable game that you both enjoy (or could learn together). Take it with you on outings and vacations so that you always have a relaxing way to share time together.
- The next time you arrive home, go find him, give him a big hug and kiss, say his name, and tell him how much you've missed him.

- Ask him to go lingerie shopping with you to help you pick out the perfect bedroom outfit.
- Invite him on a date to do something he enjoys.
- Invite him to an evening alone with you at home. Arrive before he does, and prepare a sensuous atmosphere. Prepare yourself as well.
- Put down that book (or magazine or newspaper or report) when he gets into bed next to you.
- Give him a good-night kiss.
- Say, "I love you," without expecting any words from him in return.

9

Deciphering His Desires

What does your partner desire in romance?

This chapter outlines the information you need to romance him the way *he* wants you to. You should be able to find answers to most of the questions just by listening to your partner's day-to-day conversation and by watching his responses to what you try. To answer some of the questions, however, you may have to ask him directly. You might even make a game of it: pretend that you are a sociologist, that there's no relationship, that you're simply doing a study.

By the way, there are no right answers.

Romantic Identity

- In the family in which your partner grew up, who was in charge? How were decisions made? How was affection expressed? How were conflicts resolved? Ask your partner in what ways he is similar to and different from his father. What does this mean for your relationship?
- What special things have you done for your partner that he has particularly appreciated? What makes him smile?
- In which of his abilities or qualities does he take pride? Do you compliment him on these things?
- Which of the special times the two of you have spent together has he particularly enjoyed? Which does he still remember fondly?

- Does your partner feel that he is your first priority? If not, what can you do to help him know that he is?
- What helps him relax?
- What makes him laugh?
- When you first met, what did he find special about you?
- What sort of romantic games did you play while courting? Can you bring back some of those activities to enliven your relationship today?
- Do you flirt with him on a regular basis? What is his response?
- Thinking back on when the two of you first met, what were some of the things he said he was looking forward to in your relationship?
- What has he thanked you for doing for him?
- What does he complain about?
- When you are wearing or using something he gave you, do you remind him how much you appreciate it?
- What makes him feel loved?
- What do you especially appreciate about him: what do you enjoy most about the way he looks, the way he acts, his personality, his sexuality, what he does professionally, what he does for you, and what he does for others?
- Do you compliment him on those things that you appreciate?
- Does he ever question your love for him? What specifically makes him anxious about this? How can you help him know that you truly love him?
- Do you ever say or do anything that might be interpreted as a lack of respect for what he does or says?
- Has he ever commented on things other couples do that he considers particularly loving or romantic?
- Has he ever asked you to do something romantic for him? What was it?
- Which of your personal habits annoy him?
- Which of your personal qualities does he find most appealing?

- Are you hesitant about trying some of the things that you think might please your partner? If so, is this because you fear rejection or because you would be uncomfortable doing them?
- Are you willing to experiment with new activities that might be fun for both of you?

Communication

- Do you greet your partner each time either of you arrives home?
- Do you understand his communication style? If not, how can you improve your understanding?
- Do you listen to his ideas?
- Are you clear in telling him what you want?
- Do you verbalize your appreciation for what he does for you?
- When you speak to him about little difficulties in your life, how does he respond? Does he try to solve your problems, or does he become upset when you complain about problems he cannot solve? Have you let him know what you expect or need from him in these instances?
- Has he ever accused you of nagging or henpecking him? If so, how can you let him know what you would like from him without causing that reaction?
- Are there particular topics he would like to avoid discussing? Why?
- At what times of the day, or under what circumstances, is he most receptive to your thoughts and ideas?
- What would he like to hear about himself? Is he unaware of a certain wonderful quality, or would he like to be praised for an ability he has worked to develop?
- What topics of conversation does he most enjoy?
- What topics cause disagreements between the two of you? What does he expect you to do when there are disagreements?

- Does he share his problems and concerns about various aspects of his life? Have you done or said anything that has caused him to close down communication on such issues? How can you help him open up to share with you?
- Is there anything you do (or don't do) that particularly angers or upsets him?
- Do you write love notes for him to find when you're not around?
- Can you sit silently with him for an extended period of time?
- Have you told him lately that you love him?

Sex

- What kind of relaxation gets your partner in the mood for sex?
- Does he enjoy a good massage? Do you know how to give one?
- What type of music does he consider romantic or sexy?
- Do you actively participate in sex with him?
- Have you ever done something special for him sexually that he particularly appreciated?
- Does he feel that you initiate sex often enough?
- Has he ever shown disappointment in your reaction to his sexual requests or behavior? Did this involve something that you might be willing to do under the right circumstances?
- How does he feel about his body? Do these feelings impact his sexual enjoyment?
- What circumstances have helped make sex special in the past?
- What sort of atmosphere or setting helps you feel sexy? Do you attempt to arrange this, so that you will enjoy sex as well?
- In what places is he most receptive to sex? In what places are you most receptive? If they aren't the same, is there a way to reach common ground?

- What style of clothing does he find sexy on you? What clothes does he not like on you? Will wearing a certain type of clothing make *you* feel sexier?
- Does he enjoy having food and drink before, during, and/or after sex? Do you? Have you arranged for these things to be readily available?
- Has he ever tried to change the lighting in order to make the atmosphere more conducive to sex? What sort of lighting does he prefer?
- Would special sheets (perhaps satin or flannel) make sex more exciting for him? For you?
- Does he like to watch you undress? Have you tried doing a striptease for him?
- Recall some of the best sexual experiences you've had with your partner. Are there similarities among them in terms of place, time, or other circumstances? Can you re-create these or similar circumstances in the future?
- Does he enjoy watching erotic videos or looking at erotic photos as part of a sexual experience? Are these things that you enjoy as well? Have you ever brought such materials home to share with him?
- Does he feel that you want him? How can you let him know that you want him sexually?
- Does he complain either that you don't want sex enough or that you want sex too much?
- Has he ever asked you to do anything special or different to sexually arouse him?
- Has he ever complained about your sex life? What specifically bothers him? Are his requests reasonable? Are you willing to change your behavior in order to meet his sexual needs? If not, have you discussed your romantic identity with him?
- Would he be comfortable sharing sexual fantasies with you? Would you be comfortable sharing some of yours?
- Do you have a variety of lovemaking styles that you practice together (e.g., a quickie style, a slow style, an experimental style)? What are his favorite styles? What are yours?

- Do you know specifically what gives him sexual pleasure?
- Does he respond to playfulness?
- Does he like you to talk while making love? Are you comfortable saying the words that excite him?
- Is there anything about his sexual approach or style that inhibits you or turns you off? Have you discussed this with him?
- Does he enjoy talking dirty? Are you comfortable with that? If not, have you told him?
- Have you told him your own sexual desires? Have you encouraged him to engage in the sexual styles, positions, and timing that give you the most pleasure?

Time

- How does your partner like to relax in the evening? If you don't share this time and activity with him, would he enjoy your doing so, or would he rather be alone?
- Do you allow him quiet time alone on a regular basis?
- How does he like to relax on weekends?
- Which of your vacations together has he most enjoyed?
- Which of the activities you have shared have you most enjoyed?
- Has he indicated interest in an activity that he would like to share with you—something you currently do without him, something he does, or something new to both of you?
- Could you suggest any new activities to try together?
- Have you set aside a time to spend alone with him on a regular basis? What does he enjoy doing during this time?
- Do you take time for romance every day?
- Does he feel that you spend enough quality time alone with him? How would he like to spend this time?
- Does he have enough free time for himself? What could you do to allow him more free time?
- Does he feel he's in good health? If not, what can you do to encourage him to pursue activities that would benefit his health?

- Does he feel that you're in good health? If not, what would he change about your lifestyle to make you healthier?
- Would he appreciate a surprise visit from you at work to invite him out for lunch? Do you know his work schedule so that you can plan spontaneous events during the day?
- Does your community offer inexpensive entertainment that he would enjoy (e.g., ball games, community theater, concerts in the park)?
- What kind of films does he like to see? When you go together to a movie theater or video rental store (or when you preview your choices on cable TV), who selects the film?
- What is his favorite kind of food? What varieties of wine or beer does he enjoy?
- What types of dishes would he like you to cook for him? What are you capable of cooking? Is cooking an interest you could pursue together?
- Ask him to describe a romantic evening at home; then ask him to describe a romantic evening out.
- Ask him to describe a romantic weekend together.
- Ask him to describe a romantic dream vacation.
- Does he feel that the two of you take enough time for short vacations alone together (e.g., weekend getaways)?
- Could you pack for your partner? Do you know what he needs for a weekend trip? Or would he rather pack for himself?
- Do you take vacations at places where you can be alone together at least part of the time? What would he like to do on a vacation?
- What sort of restaurants does he most enjoy? What type of food? What kind of atmosphere? What does he particularly enjoy about his favorite restaurant?
- What special date would he most enjoy? Going to a restaurant, theater, museum, or amusement park? Watching or participating in a sport?

- Do you present your best self to him (rather than saving it for others)?
- Do you pay attention to his interests? Can you discuss his work with him?
- Do you keep yourself informed about news events that he might like to discuss?
- Do you plan special time alone with your partner?
- When you are away from him on a business trip or visiting others, do you keep in contact through regular phone calls and love notes?
- Do you have interests outside the home that allow you to bring something new back to the relationship?
- Are you willing to ask your partner for help with your work-related responsibilities? With your home-related responsibilities? Can you do this without leading him to believe that you're asking him to take responsibility for your problems?

Gifts and Occasions

- What occasions are most important to your partner?
- If you gave him a book of coupons for special favors to redeem as he pleased, what sorts of things would he like you to do?
- Does he like to be surprised with spur-of-the-moment getaways, or would he rather be in on the planning?
- Have you ever caught him looking at something he would like to have from a store or catalog?
- Which of your gifts has he appreciated more than others or used often?
- Does he use tools?
- Is he involved in a sport or hobby that requires special equipment or clothing that you could purchase for him?
- Has he mentioned something for his car that he would like?
- Are there personal items related to his business or career that you could give to him (e.g., briefcase, pen, clothing)?
- What type of stores does he like to shop in? What catches his eye?

- What small surprises would he appreciate receiving for no special reason?
- Does he like the clothing that you buy for him, or would he rather you took him shopping so that he (or both of you) could choose? What are his shirt, pants, and jacket sizes?
- Does he wear jewelry? Has he ever admired men's jewelry?
- What is his favorite scent? Is it available in cologne, after-shave, soap, lotion? Would he use such products?
- What kind of music does he enjoy? Does he use cassettes, CDs, or records?

Once you have discovered what your partner wants in romance, you might want to review various sections of the book for ideas about satisfying some of these previously hidden desires. When you follow through on what you learn, you will please your partner and intensify the romance in your relationship. And you can be sure that such personal attention will encourage him to romance you in return.

Happy romancing!

Appendix

Survey Results

The survey for the book *How to Romance the Man You Love—The Way He Wants You To* was distributed through U.S. mail as well as over electronic mail (on the World Wide Web). It was carried out over a period of four months during the spring and summer of 1995.

More than 300 men across the United States and Canada responded to the survey. They ranged in age from twenty to over sixty years old. About 25 percent of survey respondents were between the ages of twenty and thirty, 45 percent were between thirty and forty, and the remaining 30 percent were over forty years old. About 25 percent were single; 75 percent were married, divorced, or widowed. A third of respondents had children living at home.

Highlights of the responses to specific statements as well as excerpts of quotes elicited by open-ended questions are presented and analyzed throughout this book.

Importance of Specific Actions

The survey asked men to rate the importance of statements that began with "I would appreciate it if my partner would . . . " The statements describing the partner's actions are presented here in order of importance.

STATEMENTS RATED IMPORTANT OR VERY IMPORTANT
BY SURVEY RESPONDENTS
(IN DESCENDING ORDER)

Percentage of respondents rating this important or very important	*"I would appreciate it if my parner would . . ."*
90–100%	listen to my ideas be fun to be around
80–90%	listen to my concerns tell me she loves me arrange for us to be together as a family (fathers) hug me show appreciation for what I do for her show independence spend time with me away from the children pursue her own interests act playful when we are alone be supportive of my career treat me as very important in her life
70–80%	initiate sex touch me in nonsexual ways keep herself looking clean and attractive keep herself in good physical condition empathize with my feelings flirt with me act sexy when we're alone together keep in touch when we are apart
60–70%	attend to my nonsexual needs attend to my sexual needs plan activities for us together give me a massage initiate creative sexual encounters

	be on time
	give me free time away without complaint
50–60%	dress nicely when we go out
	participate in my hobbies or interests
	contribute to our financial well-being
	create a sexy atmosphere when we're alone
	show off her body for me
	wear sexy lingerie for me
40–50%	help me feel masculine, protective, helpful
	laugh at my jokes
	call me during the day to say hello
	surprise me with special favors
	greet me with a special hello
	act sexy toward me when we're out
	know I'm not always in the mood for sex
	bathe with me
30–40%	advise me on what to wear
	cook enjoyable meals on a regular basis
	take the lead in keeping a clean home

Importance of Gifts and Celebrations

Survey respondents generally considered gifts and celebrations to be less important than actions. Here are the gifts that at least 50 percent of male survey respondents rated "desirable" or "very desirable," listed in descending order of desirability:

- Romantic evenings together (in or out)
- Romantic weekends together (home or away)
- Love notes
- Photos of her
- Small surprises for no reason
- Mementos of time together
- Things she makes for me
- Clothing
- Hobby or sporting equipment

Meaning of Romance

The survey asked, "When you think of romance, what words come to mind?" Answers ranged from the traditional to the intimately sensual. Here are some examples of individual responses:

- Time, commitment, love
- Trust, fun, sexy
- Wild abandonment, giving over to the emotional, dropping the intellectual, cuddling
- Love, sex, caring, togetherness, emotional support, strong feelings between two people, accepting each other as they are
- Fun, excitement, passion, curiosity, adventure, generosity
- Quiet, relaxed times with just my wife and me
- Candles, picnics, horses, silk, pillows, sunsets
- Candlelight, eyes, lying next to, poetry, laughing together, trees and fields, touching, holding hands
- Spontaneity, fun
- Affection, appreciation, trust, warmth, feeling
- Sex, privacy, time, warm, no pressure
- Touch, desire, understanding, nurturing
- Inspiration, creativity, playfulness, curiosity
- Mystery, surprise, exotic, sensual, sexy
- Emotional honesty, intimacy, wonderful and passionate sex, sharing ideas and plans, touching and sharing after sex, candlelight dinners, late-night summer walks, watching the sunset with a glass of wine in hand
- Passion, intensity, warmth, playfulness, unpredictability, newness
- Skin, lighting, whisper, candle, food, massage
- Dark, naked, private, warm, slightly tipsy, tactile, firelight, enthusiastic, emotionally secure, gentle
- Commitment, openness, communication, respect, honor, passion, tenderness, warmth, happiness, joy
- Veronica (my wife)

- Sex, love, flirtation, sensual, intimate, tenderness, sweet disposition, ecstasy
- Creativity, compassion

Romantic Interferences

Men were in accord about the things that get in the way of romance: the fundamental cause of sidelined romance is dealing with everyday life. Here are some examples from individual respondents:

- Lack of time, being tired, being too busy for even the minor touching
- Time, responsibilities
- Being in a bad mood, insecurity
- Responsibility to the household
- Business commitments, stress, preoccupation
- Embarrassment, lack of communications
- Outside distractions and worries, also internal (personal) conflicts and fears
- Children, other family members, money
- Day-to-day chores, lack of time
- Real life, fear of looking absurd
- Criticism, whining, lack of appreciation
- Work, jealousy, and money
- Phone calls and company
- Lack of communication, lack of a sense of humor, and lack of assertiveness
- Telephone calls, bill payments, and Fluffy the cat
- Work, work, and more work
- Stress, one or the other just not in the mood, time constraints, job pressures
- Children and work, financial limitations, overexpectations when we do get away
- Career, financial status, social status
- Illness, money matters, schedule conflicts, running around
- Interruptions, unwanted noise

- Just about everything
- Everybody else
- Work and other demands on each others time, and routine things like washing up and cleaning
- Fear
- Everyday life, lack of energy
- Work, bills, taxes
- Stress from jobs or other situations, lack of communication about problems or concerns, failure to say how you really feel, uncommunicated goals, not allowing enough time to deal with everyday life. Romance is important, but you have to buy groceries and fix the house sometimes, too.

Romantic Fantasy

In response to the open-ended question "What is your romantic fantasy?" men of every age and marital status described a desire to be alone with their sweetheart in a private, usually remote place. Recurrent locales were tropical islands, ocean beaches, mountains (camping trips), and luxurious hotels.

Food and scenery play major roles, but more important is the idea that the woman is open to new adventures, including sensual and sexual ones. Because men view the trivial concerns of everyday living as the major obstacle to romance, they want their partner to be able to let go of daily anxieties and focus on the dream getaway.

Numerous quotes from the responses to this question are presented throughout the book.

Special Actions

The survey asked, "Has there ever been a time when a partner made you feel really special?" Responses told of fun that a partner created; special occasions, such as birthdays; and sex, specifically times when the woman took the initiative. Here are some examples:

- She makes me laugh. She makes me feel special. I love how she looks and how she looks at me.
- Yes. She took the attitude of pleasing me first. [She was] willing to do whatever I wanted to do.
- Yes. When I was told I was a good lover.
- Promotions, birthdays, retirement.
- Whenever I feel like the world is falling apart around me, she lifts my spirits.
- My girlfriend has a very good opinion about me, and she lets everyone know every chance she gets.
- I remember that my lover once surprised me with a weekend trip to a health spa. She never told me where we were going. She had told me to keep the weekend open and picked me up from work with everything we needed.
- She told me that, had she been my previous lover, she would have never let me go.
- When she lets me know that I've satisfied her sexual needs.
- Whenever she seduces me!
- Yes. When she let me know I was a good lover.
- Gifts that were given for no reason.
- For our sixth anniversary, my wife "kidnapped" me: she arranged a weekend at a bed-and-breakfast on the coast.
- Yes. When she gave up other things to be with me just because she wanted to.
- Often, she tells me how wonderful I am whenever I do something nice for her.
- When it was my birthday she took me out—total surprise. That evening was all mine to do whatever I wanted. That was great.
- Yes. Usually when I have had a very stressful day at work my wife will give me a massage, and I find this very special.
- When she acts very sexy toward me in public.
- Yes. Occasionally, after we make love, she tells me that she feels very lucky, that I am really something else. This makes me feel great, feeds my male ego!
- Yes. A surprise party on a thirtieth birthday.

- Complimenting me to her friends when I'm not around.
- She would occasionally dress in sexy costumes with a fantasy ready to "perform" when I came home from work.
- When I've come home and found my wife sitting on the couch wearing lingerie with a glass of wine ready for me.
- Yes. Mostly when she showed a great deal of real appreciation for something I did for her. It made me feel like I was a nice person for having thought of it.
- The most wonderful Welcome Home card when I'd been away.
- Birthday surprise party.
- Trip for two with dinner.
- Small actions I find romantic include attention to me, kind words.
- Hot springs nude under stars.
- Whenever she tells me she loves me.
- Planning our future together.
- When she wrote a song about being together. It made me feel trusted.
- When I came home midweek, tired from work, and she greeted me at the door wearing nothing but a smile.
- She planned a whole evening together.
- When a partner let me know that I had given her intense pleasure.
- Yes. She complimented me in ways that helped build my self-confidence and emphasized that I could relax and "be me" and she would enjoy whatever happened without pretense.

Personal Suggestions

In response to "If my partner would/would not . . . , we would have a better relationship," survey respondents' numerous suggestions dealt with the specific circumstances of their own relationships. These responses were used in the book only where there were patterns and consistencies. Here are some of the desires expressed:

- Need for more open communication, honesty.
- Need for partner to accept herself and not try to change to please others.
- Would not make assumptions about me or what I think or how I am, would give me credit for the things I have done, and have not done.
- Consider what has actually been said, done, or has happened before being defensive or angry.
- If she would tell me how she feels or any problems she has (with me).
- If she had displayed that she was unhappy, some of our problems might have been solved.
- The only thing I can say is: if she wouldn't worry so much about her job; she's very dedicated and works very hard, but it leaves her exhausted and stressed. Other than that, we're doing well.
- Be more assertive about her own needs.
- Not be late for dates.
- Be more open and honest.
- Take better care of her body.
- Be more creative in all things.
- I would like my partner to be a little more confident about herself and take my compliments more seriously.
- Would honor me and hold me in higher esteem/would not focus on what she doesn't like about me.
- If my partner would figure out what it is she wants, exactly. You can't have something if you don't know what it is you want.
- Take initiative in the role of the romancer (I personally enjoy romancing, but would like to be romanced once in a while, too).
- If she would let me know her feelings.
- If my partner would consider my feelings, we would have a better relationship.

- Tell me when things I do bother her.
- Not leave all decisions up to me. She should take the initiative sometimes and be more creative about things.
- If she would just relax a little more.
- I think she's perfect. I am one lucky dog.
- If she was more comfortable with her body.
- If she had a life away from her family.
- Be a little less forceful and pushy in our personal dealings. This trait serves her well in her business relationships but can lead to strained feelings when applied around the house.
- Spend more time talking, as well as developing more interests of her own.
- If she would manage her finances better, we would have a better relationship.
- Just take more time for us away from the kids, so we could rekindle our love for one another. The focus and center of the family needs to be us and how we treat and feel about one another.
- If she would do more to please me during sex.
- I wish she would either temper her expectations or let people know what she expects of them.
- Would appreciate my career despite my income; would acknowledge the things I do for her.
- Learn that she is not the only one that needs to be reassured that they are an important part of the relationship.
- It would be nice for her to make love to me instead of me being the one that is "required" to do it to her.
- Would not be so concerned about what others think, or about what she thinks I or others think.
- She's perfect.
- Never, ever show jealousy.
- Would keep in shape.
- Would not wash my socks and white shirts in the same wash load.
- If my partner would be more assertive and vocal about what her sexual needs are, we would have a better rela-

tionship. A lot of my sense of value in my marriage comes from being able to satisfy my wife sexually.

- Loosen up and let go of prior inhibitions.
- It would be better if we had more interests in common.
- Think and be able to take part in an intelligent conversation.
- Would write me more explicit love letters/would not appear ambivalent about me.
- More initiation on her part.
- Would communicate more. Be more independent when we are apart and be more interdependent when we are together, but never be anything less than her own person.
- Not imagine that I can read her thoughts. Not assume that something I said once is still how I feel now.
- Appreciate (and express appreciation for) the things I do to try to provide for and protect you. If these things aren't important to you, tell me what is so I can try to adjust and provide value to you.
- Listen more carefully.

References

Betcher, William. *Intimate Play* (New York, NY: Penguin Books, 1988).

Bly, Robert. *Iron John: A Book About Men* (New York, NY: Vintage Books, 1992).

Connell, Evan S. *Mr. Bridge* (New York, NY: Alfred A. Knopf, 1969).

Gray, John. *Mars and Venus in the Bedroom* (New York, NY: HarperCollins, 1995).

Gray, John. *Men Are from Mars, Women Are from Venus* (New York, NY: HarperCollins, 1992).

Keen, Sam. *Fire in the Belly: On Being a Man* New York, NY: Bantam Books, 1991).

Kingma, Daphne Rose. *The Men We Never Knew* (Berkeley, CA: Conari Press, 1994).

Peck, M. Scott. *The Road Less Traveled* (New York, NY: Simon & Schuster, 1978).

Sanna, Lucy, with Kathy Miller. *How to Romance the Woman You Love—The Way She Wants You To!* (Rocklin, CA: Prima Publishing, 1995).

Smith, Gerald. *Couple Therapy* (New York, NY: Collier Books, 1974).

Stoppard, Miriam. *The Magic of Sex* (New York, NY: Dorling Kindersley, 1992).

Tannen, Deborah. *That's Not What I Meant: How Conversational Style Makes or Breaks Relationships* (New York,NY: William Morrow and Company, 1990).

Tannen, Deborah. *You Just Don't Understand: Women and Men in Conversation* (New York, NY: William Morrow and Company, 1990).

Zilbergeld, Bernie. *The New Male Sexuality* (New York, NY: Bantam Books, 1992).

Index

Women Reveal Their Romantic Desires

Inside this book are powerful strategies for creating romance every day.
Based on substantial research, this
book reveals the most intimate
desires of women from across the
country. It includes dozens of stimulating strategies and imaginative suggestions to help fulfill the potential
of a first date or renew the thrill in a
lifelong love.

ISBN 0-7615-0870-8
Paperback / 224 pages
U.S. $12.95 / Can. $19.95

Great Dates, FUN Dates—for Less!

Let's face it: Coming up with a creative yet affordable night out can be a challenge. But there are ways to put a charge in your dating life without putting a big charge on your credit card. If you're looking for entertaining, adventurous, or just plain fun dating ideas that won't break the bank, this refreshing guide is your ideal companion. Inside you'll find new ideas for:

- Fun and frugal dates
- Romantic dates
- Sport and leisure dates
- Outdoor dates
- And much more!

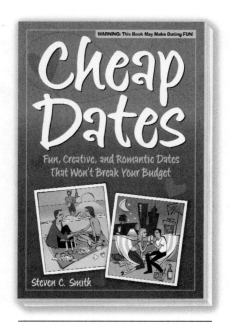